Children's Advent Stories for Bedtime

OTHER BOOKS BY JULIE AND DAVID LAVENDER

Raising Good Sons: Christian Parenting Principles for Nurturing Boys of Faith and Character

Jumbo Bible Word Search: Stimulate Your Mind and Grow in Faith

Children's Bible Stories for Bedtime: To Grow in Faith and Love

Strength for All Seasons: A Mom's Devotional of Powerful Verses and Prayers

Children's Advent Stories for Bedtime

CELEBRATE THE TRUE MEANING OF CHRISTMAS

Julie & David Lavender

Illustrated by Shahar Kober

Z KIDS • NEW YORK

Z Kids
An imprint of Zeitgeist™
A division of Penguin Random House LLC
1745 Broadway, New York, NY 10019
zeitgeistpublishing.com
penguinrandomhouse.com

ISBN: 9798217151493
Ebook ISBN: 9798217151486

Manufactured in China

1st Printing

Illustrations by Shahar Kober
Book design by Aimee Fleck
Author photograph © by Bruce Morrissey of Smuggsphoto.com
Edited by Kim Suarez

The authorized representative in the EU for product safety and compliance is Penguin Random House Ireland, Morrison Chambers, 32 Nassau Street, Dublin D02 YH68, Ireland. https://eu-contact.penguin.ie

Note to Readers: The stories in this book are retellings of stories contained in the Bible and should not take the place of direct Scripture. They are meant to aide in children's greater understanding of the Bible and its messages, using a tone and language ideal for that age group.

To our children, Jeremy, Jenifer, Jeb Daniel, and Jessica, who make every Christmas season special; to our sons-in-love, Adam and Dawson; and to our grandchildren, Benaiah, Maverick, and Danae, who make Christmas even sweeter

Contents

INTRODUCTION

Jesus is coming! For many years and lots of generations, God promised to send a Savior to take away the sins of the world. God's people anxiously anticipated the arrival of the Savior. How much longer? When would Jesus arrive? The people lived with hope for the Savior and longed for the peace and joy and love he would bring to the world.

Are you anticipating the birth of Jesus this season? Are you celebrating his first arrival many years ago and anxiously preparing for his second coming?

The true meaning of Christmas isn't about chaotic shopping days, the busyness of the season, and waiting for Santa. Rather, the blessed and glorious meaning of the season is the birth of God's Son, the one who would change the world forever.

The twenty-five Advent bedtime stories included in this book celebrate Jesus' birth on the days that lead to Christmas Day. Fall asleep with a heart and mind full of hope for the one to come.

The stories relate to Jesus' birth, dive into God's Word, and point to God's gift. Bible studies reinforce the gospel message and bring understanding to God's Word. Reflection thoughts and questions connect what you've read to your own life. And a prayer at the end encourages conversation with God, the giver of the greatest gift of all on Christmas morning.

GETTING READY FOR BEDTIME

Bedtime during the Christmas season can be especially challenging—extra holiday events on the calendar, great anticipation for the days ahead, and lots to mark off on the to-do list.

The busyness of this time of year is an even greater reason for you to get a good night's rest. Healthy sleep habits give you the energy you need for another day of learning, playing, enjoying the season, and drawing closer to God. A good night's rest prepares you for the day ahead and keeps you cheerful with family and friends during the frenzy of the holidays.

Here are twelve ways to keep a jolly Christmas mood and settle down for a long winter's nap . . . well, one that lasts through the night, anyway.

1. **Talk to your parents or guardians about having a family movie night soon.** Pick a favorite Christmas movie to watch together. Start the movie so that it ends at least one hour before bedtime since screen time excites the brain and prevents your body from getting sleepy.
2. **Get ready for bed with bath, pj's, and teeth-brushing.** Then gather and talk about family Christmas traditions and how they got started. Ask your parents to add any must-dos to the holiday schedule.

3. **Tidy your room because a clean room calms the brain.** Then talk as a family about each person's favorite holiday decorations or ornaments. Find out why that decoration or ornament is a favorite.
4. **Organize the clothes and supplies you'll need for the next day.** Once everything is handy and in an easy-to-find location, ask Mom or Dad if they need any help wrapping gifts or making holiday preparations.
5. **After one last drink of water, talk with Mom or Dad about holiday baking plans.** What's your favorite Christmas cookie? Favorite Christmas snack? Make plans to bake together and share goodies with others.
6. **If it's not quite time for bed yet, ask if you can listen to Christmas music as a family.** Choose a few upbeat holiday favorites first, and end with some calming Christmas tunes.
7. **For a festive moment before bedtime, ask if the family can add a few more tinsel strands to the Christmas tree.** Each time a family member adds a piece of tinsel, have them share something they are thankful for.
8. **Does your family hang mistletoe for the holidays?** Give family members bedtime hugs and kisses on the cheek before retiring for the evening.

9. **Set up the Nativity scene.** Take turns placing each piece. Reserve baby Jesus for the final piece, and draw straws to see who gets to place baby Jesus on the manger.
10. **Just before saying prayers together, remember and talk about Christmases of the past spent with relatives and close friends.** Pray for extended family members.
11. **Does your family create gingerbread houses this time of year?** Make up a bedtime story about living in a house made of candy and sweet treats.
12. **Wear your cheer.** Dress in matching holiday pajamas with your family, ensuring that everyone can take in the comfort of the season.

DECEMBER 1

God Has a Plan

JOHN 1:1–5; GENESIS 1–3

A very long time ago, nothing existed. No plants. No animals. No sky or mountains or rivers. No stars or planets or moon. Nothing but God.

The Bible says that God exists as one being but in three distinct forms: the Father, the Son—Jesus—and the Holy Spirit. Together, they are called the Trinity.

When God made the heavens and everything on earth into being, Jesus was with him. As the Trinity, God did this in just six days.

The earth was empty, and darkness covered everything. When God spoke the words "Let there be light," that's exactly what happened—light shone everywhere! God separated the light from the darkness and called the light "day." He called the darkness "night." God said the light was good! This was Day 1 of God's creation.

On Day 2, God created the sky. And guess what? God said the sky was good.

On Day 3, God gathered the water below the sky and called the water "seas." When God formed the seas, dry ground appeared. He called the dry ground "land."

God said this was good.

Also on the third day, God caused the land to grow all sorts of vegetation—lush, green plants; trees with gobs of apples, peaches, and plums; and fields of soft green grass.

On Day 4, God created the sun, the moon, and the stars. He made the sun to shine during the day and the moon and stars to appear at night.

And you know what? Just like all his other creations, God saw that they were good too.

On Day 5, God created the animals of the water and the animals of the air. He filled the oceans and seas and ponds with dolphins, crabs, octopuses, and sharks. Flying above the earth, feathered animals appeared, from eagles and hawks to parakeets and pigeons—God made them all and saw that it was good.

On Day 6, God created animals that moved on the land—cats and dogs, frogs and toads, spiders and ladybugs, raccoons and porcupines, lions and giraffes.

And finally, last but not least, on Day 6, God created humans. Man appeared first, and God named him Adam. He then created a woman and named her Eve. Adam and Eve lived in a beautiful garden called Eden. And I bet you can't guess what God said about Adam and Eve. God said his creation of humankind was *very* good.

The world was perfect. Perfectly beautiful. Perfectly created. Perfect in every way.

God gave Adam instructions to take care of the earth, and the humans could enjoy and live off the fruit and vegetables of the land. But God warned them not to eat from one particular tree: the Tree of the Knowledge of Good and Evil. With all the other sources of food, you would think that they wouldn't be tempted to eat from that tree. Unfortunately, Adam and Eve disobeyed God.

Satan, God's enemy, took the form of a serpent and tricked Eve. The serpent talked Eve into taking the fruit from the Tree of the Knowledge of Good and Evil, and Eve shared the fruit with Adam.

By disobeying God, Adam and Eve sinned. They knew they were wrong for eating the forbidden fruit. They tried to hide from God, but God sees and knows all.

Adam and Eve had to face the consequences and take responsibility for their wrongdoing. God told them they could not stay in the Garden of Eden, and so they were forced to leave the beautiful, perfect garden he had created for them. (As for the serpent, God told him that from now on, he would have to crawl on his belly.)

Right then and there, God announced he had a plan. He promised he would send someone perfect who would never sin. This someone would save all the humans that would ever inhabit the earth. He knew we would need rescuing and that someone had to pay the price for our sins. That special someone?

His Son, Jesus.

Bible Study

When Adam and Eve disobeyed God, sin was introduced into the world. Sometimes we call their sin "original sin," because it was the first time sin happened. That meant every generation—every person born after Adam and Eve—was born into a sinful world.

Besides the original sin of Adam and Eve, every human being also has their own personal sins. We all sin with our words and our actions. We can never be perfect. It's just too hard. We live in a fallen, imperfect world, and we make mistakes . . . every day . . . sometimes lots of times each day.

But God knew this would happen. He knew how hard it would be to be perfect. He knew we wouldn't always make the right choices. He knew we would need someone to save us from our sins.

That's where God's Son, Jesus, comes into the story. Jesus is God's perfect, sinless Son. Jesus is part of the Trinity and was with God in the beginning.

And, at just the right time, God would send his Son to earth to be born as a baby, grow up, and become the Savior of the whole world. To be the light of the world. To take away the darkness of our sin so that if we believe in him as God's one and only Son, we can one day live in heaven with God forever. The world needed Jesus then. The world needs Jesus now.

Reflection

- Why do you think Adam and Eve disobeyed God? Do you sometimes disobey your parents or your teachers?
- When you sin with your words or your actions, how does that make you feel? Do you think your sin affects other people? What should you do after you sin?
- Jesus came to earth to show us how to live. He came to earth so that we could be forgiven of our sins. What words do you use when you talk to Jesus about your sins?

Prayer

Dear God, thank you for creating this beautiful world for us to live in. Your creations are magnificent. Thank you, especially, for sending your Son, Jesus, to take away the sins of the world. You knew we needed Jesus to come here, first as a baby and then to grow up to be the Savior of the world. Thank you, God. Amen.

DECEMBER 2

A Savior Is Coming

DANIEL 2:44, 7:13–14, MICAH 5:2–5; ISAIAH 7:14, 9:6–7

During the days of the Bible, when God had a message for his people, he often revealed that message through a person called a prophet. A prophet's purpose was to share God's message and God's words with others.

At times, the message was something like: "Stop sinning and do what is right and good."

At other times, the message warned the people that their land would soon fall into the hands of another empire. But God promised he would never leave his people.

Another time, God wanted his prophet to tell the people to stop worshiping false gods. God said, "Worship only me, the one true God."

God used prophets like messengers to spread the word and make sure people knew God's words and warnings.

But the most exciting message God gave prophets to share with people was this announcement: "Jesus is coming."

God wanted us to know he had a plan to save the world. At just the right time, he would send his Son, Jesus, to be the light of the world.

In the Old Testament, a long time before Jesus was born, the prophet Daniel announced that Jesus would come. Daniel explained that God had a plan from the beginning of creation: "The God of heaven will set up a kingdom that will never be destroyed."

Daniel made sure people knew that God promised to send his Son, Jesus the Messiah, to take away our sins. Jesus would grow to be a man and tell others about his Father in heaven. Jesus would come to the earth to save us from our sins. Daniel announced to everyone who would listen about Jesus' coming.

Another prophet in the Old Testament told people about Jesus. Micah proclaimed Jesus would be born in Bethlehem. Micah spoke these words from God, saying Jesus will "stand and shepherd his flock in the strength of the Lord, in the majesty of the name of the Lord his God."

Micah also said, "And he will be our peace."

Micah foretold Jesus' birth. That means he told other people about it a long time before it happened. And he made sure people knew that it would be Jesus who would make a way for our sins to be forgiven.

Another prophet, Isaiah, told God's people a lot about Jesus. Isaiah reminded God's people that God promised a long time ago that he would send his Son, Jesus, to establish God's kingdom.

Isaiah foretold the birth of Jesus when he told God's people that a young girl who had never been married would give birth to a son. Isaiah said, "And he will be called Immanuel."

Immanuel means "God is with us." The Bible uses "Immanuel" as another way to refer to Jesus.

Throughout the Old Testament, God's prophets reminded people about two important promises. The first big promise God wanted the people to know is this: God is always with us. God never leaves us. No matter how dark it may seem, no matter what difficulty or problem we face, God never leaves our side. He promises to always be with us.

And the second big, huge, important promise God shared through the prophets is this: God has a plan to send his Son, Jesus, to save the world. At just the right time, God would send his Son to earth to become the Savior of the world.

That Savior is Jesus, God's one and only Son.

People anticipated—which means looked forward to—the Advent of Jesus the Messiah. "Advent" means "coming." They didn't know when it would happen, but they longed for the day Jesus would be born.

God had a plan, and it involved a little baby.

The world needed Jesus. Come, Lord Jesus. Come, baby Jesus.

Bible Study

Sometimes the people who lived in the days of the Bible forgot about God's promises. They forgot God promised to send his Son, Jesus, to take away the sins of the world. The people often made bad choices and kept sinning. They didn't choose to do what was right.

God used prophets, good people who loved God and tried really hard to do what was right, to remind people of his promise to send his Son. God told the prophets to tell people to stop sinning and make good choices.

God also wanted the prophets to remind people God is always with them. Even when times got hard, the prophets told people not to forget about God, because he was always right there with them, despite the difficult things happening.

When you face challenges or tough times, you can remember that God loves you so much that he promises to never leave you—not ever! God is always by your side. We can trust those promises because God always keeps his promises.

He will always love us, and he will always be with us. God is just a prayer away. He's there for you, no matter what.

And just like the people back then anticipated the birth of Jesus, we can look forward to the Advent season when we celebrate his birth. The Christmas season means Jesus' birthday is coming. It's almost here.

Reflection

- What important job did prophets have in the Old Testament? What two really big promises did God tell the prophets to share with his people?
- Why did God have a plan to send his Son, Jesus, to earth? How do we know about God's plan to send Jesus? In what ways did God make his plan really clear?
- Think about a recent time when you faced a hard problem. Did you talk to God about your problem? How did God help you with that tough time?
- What helps you remember that God is always with you? Is there a friend you want to tell about God's promise to never leave you?

Prayer

Dear God, thank you for your plan to send Jesus to take away my sins and the sins of the world. Help me make good choices. Help me be obedient. Forgive me when I do wrong things that hurt you and hurt other people. Remind me you are always with me and you love me so much you thought of me when you sent Jesus. Help me look forward to celebrating your birthday this Christmas. Amen.

JEHOSHAPHAT
BOAZ
RUTH
SALMON
RAHAB
TAMAR
JUDAH
JACOB
ABRAHAM

DECEMBER 3

Not a Perfect Family

GENESIS 3, 12, 27, 31, 38; JOSHUA 2, 6; RUTH 2–4; 2 CHRONICLES 20; MATTHEW 1:1–17; LUKE 3:23–38; HABAKKUK 1:13; PSALM 101:3–8

God's Son, Jesus, lived a perfect, sinless life. He never sinned. Not even once. Jesus never ever made wrong choices. He didn't disobey God. Jesus is the only person to ever walk on earth who never did anything wrong.

This was God's plan—to send his perfect Son to earth to take on the sins of the world. That way we could be forgiven of our sins and one day live forever in heaven with God.

But while Jesus was perfect, he didn't have a perfect earthly family. Jesus' lineage—the people in his family who lived generations and generations before him—was made up of many sinful people who disobeyed God.

The books of Matthew and Luke in the New Testament list Jesus' genealogy. In other words, those books trace the people in Jesus' family all the way back to Adam, the very first person God created to live on earth.

Some of those family members were not good people. Many of them made lots of mistakes, but God never stopped loving them.

For example, do you remember that Adam and Eve disobeyed God when they ate from the Tree of the Knowledge of Good and Evil in the Garden of Eden? Adam and Eve suffered consequences because of their disobedience, but God still loved them and never stopped taking care of them. God also promised to never leave them. And Adam and Eve were part of God's plan. God used Adam and Eve to populate the entire world.

Abraham, another member of Jesus' lineage, disobeyed God a number of times. Early in Abraham's story, God told Abraham to leave his home and settle in Canaan. Instead, Abraham settled in Egypt, where food was plentiful. Abraham didn't trust God to provide what he needed.

Later, Abraham lied to a king about his wife. Abraham didn't trust God to protect him. And in another part of his story, Abraham didn't believe God's promise to give him a son.

Abraham's disobedience brought penalties and hard times for his family. But God never gave up on Abraham. God used Abraham as part of his big plan, despite Abraham's lies, disobedience, lack of trust, and disbelief in God's promises. God continued to love Abraham and take care of him. God made Abraham the father of many nations. God can use anyone to fulfill his plans, even imperfect people.

Abraham's grandson Jacob stole his brother's blessing and lied to his father, Isaac, over and over again. Jacob later cheated his uncle by taking things that didn't belong to him. Jacob also treated his family unfairly.

Even with Jacob's faults and wrongdoings, God never stopped loving him. Jacob was part of God's plan to one day send a Savior to the world. Jacob made a lot of mistakes. Tough outcomes followed his mistakes. But God still used Jacob to carry out his plan.

Judah and Tamar, also listed as members of Jesus' lineage, faced hardships and troubles of their own. Lies and trickery brought on painful results. But God didn't forget Judah and Tamar. They were part of God's plan for the lineage of Jesus.

The genealogy of Jesus includes a Canaanite woman named Rahab. Her family did not worship God. They worshiped idols and false gods. They did not trust or believe in the one true God. Yet God used Rahab to save some of his chosen people in the city of Jericho.

Rahab turned away from the false gods of her family and began trusting God. When Rahab believed in God, she became part of God's family. And when she later married Salmon and became the mother of Boaz, she became part of Jesus' lineage.

The Bible tells the story of Boaz, a good and kind man, who took care of a woman named Ruth. Boaz became Ruth's "redeemer." In Bible days, a redeemer was a person who took care of a relative in trouble or in need of help. Ruth, a woman from Moab, was not part of God's chosen people. Yet God used her as part of his big plan too.

The story of Boaz and Ruth shows us what it means to be redeemed. Jesus is our Redeemer. When we trust in Jesus, he takes care of us in our time of trouble. He's always there for us when we need help.

When Jehoshaphat, another person in Jesus' genealogy, became king of Judah, he told the people to stop worshiping false gods. He told them to worship only God. Jehoshaphat taught the people to follow God's law and trust in God.

Jesus' ancestors—some good, some not-so-good, and a few that were really bad—needed Jesus. The only person who could save them from their sins was Jesus. From the days of Adam until just before Jesus came to earth as a baby, God reminded his people he had a plan to send Jesus to save them.

The Bible is full of stories that teach us about God and Jesus. Jesus' ancestors—generations and generations of family members that go all the way back to Adam—remind us that God can use anyone to fulfill his plans.

Despite their sins, their family, their past, their mistakes, or their disobedience, God could still use them to carry out his plan for Jesus to one day come to be the Savior of the world.

Throughout each generation in Jesus' lineage, people needed a savior. God told his people, "Jesus is coming."

Bible Study

Jesus' ancestors—the generations of his family who lived before him—were imperfect people. Sometimes they made bad choices. Other times, they were good and kind and loving. The stories about Jesus' lineage, as well as all the stories in the Bible about other people, teach us about God's grace and forgiveness.

Those stories show us that no matter what we've done, who we are, or how much we've sinned, God loves us and gives us grace and forgiveness. We also know that God can use us for his plans despite our sins or wrongdoings.

If God can use people like Abraham, Tamar, Rahab, Boaz, Ruth, and Jehoshaphat, he can use us too. Even if our family isn't perfect and even if we're not perfect, we are still loved and valued by God.

Reflection

- The Bible talks about God's grace, which is what we call God's kindness. God gives us his kindness as a gift, and he never takes it away, even when we make mistakes. Think about a time you felt God's kindness.

- Many of the people in the Bible made bad choices and suffered consequences. What helps you know how to make good choices?
- When you make a bad choice that hurts God or someone you know, what can you do right away to fix your mistake?

Prayer

Dear God, forgive me when I make bad choices. Help me know right from wrong and help me make good choices. Help me choose kindness, goodness, and respect. Thank you, God, for your grace and forgiveness when I make mistakes. I'm so glad I'm in your family. Help me obey you always and show me how to do the good things you want me to do. Amen.

DECEMBER 4

A Man After God's Heart

1 SAMUEL 13–19; PSALM 23; 2 SAMUEL 11–12

Being the youngest son, David wasn't quite old enough to fight battles like his older brothers, who were fighting the Philistines, enemies of God's people. Instead, David's father, Jesse, sent the teenager on an errand to check on them.

As he got closer to the battlefield, David heard about Goliath, a fearsome giant fighting for the Philistines. Nobody wanted to face him.

Trusting that God would protect him, David said, "I'll fight the giant."

King Saul knew his fighters were no match for Goliath's size and skills, so naturally the king doubted David's ability to win this fight. Besides, David was too young. But David told him he could defeat the giant. He'd fought bears and lions while on watch as a shepherd. He said, "The Lord who rescued me from the paw of the lion and the paw of the bear will rescue me from the hand of this Philistine."

David had complete trust in God. He wasn't afraid. And with just a slingshot and a rock, David defeated the giant! When the Philistines saw that their hero was no more, they turned and ran the other way! The battle was over and everyone returned home.

While David had proved himself a skilled fighter, he also excelled at harp playing. Whenever King Saul felt troubled, he sent for David to come to the palace to play the harp.

While the music calmed King Saul, it was only momentary peace. What King Saul really needed most was the peace that came only from God. David knew that peace, but Saul did not. In fact, King Saul even tried to kill David on more than one occasion because he was jealous of David. David was a skilled fighter and a talented musician, and he trusted God. The Bible even tells us David was good-looking. It angered King Saul that the people seemed to favor David over him.

King Saul's son Jonathan was David's best friend. Jonathan did his best to save David from his father's anger. But in the same way David approached Goliath, David trusted God to protect him from King Saul. David's trust in God gave him peace, and that peace helped him be brave when King Saul threatened to kill him.

David wrote many words in the book of Psalms about the same peace that helped him when he fought the giant and when he faced an angry King Saul. His words are so poetic, many people today turn to them when they feel scared and anxious. One of the most famous verses is Psalm 23: "The LORD is my shepherd, I lack nothing . . . Even though I walk through the darkest valley, I will fear no evil, for you are with me."

Much later in David's story, he becomes the king of Israel. David trusted God to help him lead God's people. David became known as a man after God's own heart because he always wanted to obey God and do what God wanted him to do.

This didn't make David perfect. In fact, David did a terrible thing while he was king. David took a woman named Bathsheba as his wife, but Bathsheba was married to someone else. David ordered men in his army to make sure Bathsheba's husband would get killed in a battle so he could have Bathsheba for his own wife.

When God sent the prophet Nathan to point out David's sin, David repented, which means he felt sorry for what he did wrong, and he asked God to forgive him and wash away his sins and make him white as snow again. David promised to try harder to do what was right to please God.

God forgave him, and David felt this forgiveness because the shame and guilt that had been weighing him down were replaced with God's peace. No matter what happened, he never stopped worshiping God. He wrote more psalms so that others could know the importance of trusting God. David wanted people to know God's peace just like he did.

Many generations later, Jesus would be born from the same lineage as David. While David was a great king, Jesus was the

King of all Kings! Jesus wanted all his followers to feel the same peace that David felt. That's why Jesus said in John 14:27, "Peace I leave with you; my peace I give to you. Not as the world gives do I give to you. Let not your hearts be troubled, neither let them be afraid" (ESV).

Jesus is actually called the Prince of Peace. He brings peace to all who trust in him.

Bible Study

Jesus came to earth to make our relationship right with God. Because of our sin, we need Jesus to be our Savior, to take away our sins, so that we can have a personal relationship with God. Only Jesus can take away our sins and make our relationship with God right.

Jesus said in John 14:6, "I am the way, the truth, and the life. No one comes to the Father except through Me" (NKJV). Like David, "a man after God's own heart," trusting Jesus as our Lord and Savior gives us peace of mind, knowing that we have a relationship with God and that one day, we will live forever with God in heaven.

This doesn't mean we won't have trouble here on earth. In fact, Jesus told us we most definitely would face hardships in this world. But when we trust Jesus, we know this world is not our home because he's made our home for us in heaven.

When our peace and hope are in Jesus, we do not have to fear what might happen on earth. The peace we have when we trust Jesus is different than what the world might offer us. When we love God and trust Jesus as his Son, we can be sure that God will never leave us nor turn his back on us. God promises to take care of us.

Jesus gives us peace—the calm and confident assurance that we belong to God, and one day we will live forever with him in heaven.

Reflection

- Sometimes when we have a big problem, we need help from an adult we can trust. Think about a time when you had to do something really hard. Besides God, who else did you talk to about that situation?
- What advice did that person share with you about your hard task? How did God help you get through that tough situation?
- How did that hard time help you learn to trust God more? Who can you share your story with to help them trust God more? Consider drawing pictures or making a poster about the different ways God helps you.
- What situations make you nervous? How can trusting God give you peace during those times?

Prayer

Dear God, when troubles happen in this world, I sometimes get scared or anxious. Sometimes I feel like I'm facing a giant, just like David did. Help me remember that I can trust you to take care of me in those times. Help me trust you more and more each day. Thank you for sending Jesus to bring peace to the world. Please help me feel the peace of Jesus every day. Amen.

HIS NAME
IS JOHN

DECEMBER 5

God Makes the Impossible Possible

LUKE 1:5–25, 1:57–80

A long time ago, before the birth of Jesus, a man named Zechariah married a woman named Elizabeth. Zechariah and Elizabeth lived near the mountains in Judea.

Zechariah and Elizabeth were good people who loved the Lord. They worshiped God with their whole hearts. They prayed and talked to God. They followed God's commands and did what was right. They made good choices. They were kind to others.

But something was missing in their lives. The couple hoped to have a family of their own, and they prayed for children. Yet, as year after year went by, the couple remained childless, even into old age. Elizabeth was especially sad that she had no children to care for.

Zechariah was a priest in the house of the Lord. When it was his turn to serve as priest, he traveled to Jerusalem to perform his duties. Zechariah worked with other priests at the temple too.

One of the jobs of the temple priests was to burn incense. Priests mixed different spices together in a holder and lit a fire under the spices. That made the spices cook and give off a delightful smell.

The pleasant aroma rising from the incense represents a sweet offering to God. It's also a sign of reverence and dedication. Burning incense symbolizes prayers floating up to God.

The priests took turns burning incense, according to the custom of the priesthood. When it was Zechariah's turn, he went inside while the other priests prayed outside the temple.

Suddenly, the angel Gabriel appeared before Zechariah, standing near the burning incense. Zechariah was frightened. He'd never seen an angel before.

Gabriel said, "Do not be afraid, Zechariah."

But Zechariah was afraid.

Gabriel continued, "Your prayer has been heard. Your wife Elizabeth will bear you a son, and you are to call him John."

Zechariah was further told that the baby would be a joy and delight and that many people would rejoice at his birth.

"For he will be great in the sight of the Lord," Gabriel told Zechariah.

Zechariah couldn't believe what he was hearing with his own ears. He probably couldn't believe what he was seeing with his own eyes, either. An angel with good news about a son?

"How can I be sure of this? I am an old man and my wife is well along in years," Zechariah said.

Zechariah doubted Gabriel's prediction. It all seemed too good to be true. He and his wife were too old to have kids. He didn't think it could be possible.

Zechariah lacked the faith to believe the angel's words. He didn't believe God could do the impossible.

Gabriel reassured him that God's words were true. "I have been sent to speak to you and to tell you this good news. And now you will be silent and not able to speak until the day this happens, because you did not believe my words." Because Zechariah doubted, God caused him to not be able to speak until the baby was born! Can you imagine?

When Zechariah came out of the temple and tried to tell the other priests what had happened with the angel, no sound came out of his mouth! So he moved his hands and waved his arms to make signs. Yet no one could understand what he meant.

When Zechariah's temple duties were finished, he returned to Elizabeth in the hill country of Judea. And guess what. Soon, Elizabeth became pregnant.

She was so excited to be having a baby! She couldn't stop praising the Lord. "The Lord has done this for me," she said. God had shown her his favor.

In his silence, Zechariah had a lot of time to think about God and Gabriel's words. For nine months, he could not talk to anyone. He probably learned a lot about trusting God during that time. And Zechariah certainly learned that God can do impossible things that nobody else can do. Zechariah learned God can make the impossible possible.

Zechariah might have thought about God's promise to send a Savior one day. Zechariah, like so many of God's people, anxiously awaited the Messiah.

When the time came for Elizabeth to give birth to their son, everyone was so excited for the couple and shared in their joy for what the Lord had done for them.

It was the custom in those days to name a baby boy after his father, so neighbors and family members thought they would name the baby Zechariah.

"No," said Elizabeth. "He is to be called John."

The people couldn't understand why Elizabeth wanted to name the baby John when no one in their family had that name.

Neighbors and family members asked Zechariah what he wanted to name the baby. Because he still couldn't use his words to speak, he wrote these words on a tablet: "His name is John."

Right then, Zechariah's words returned. He could speak again!

And you know what he did first with his words? He praised the Lord!

Everyone who heard the story of the newborn baby John marveled at what God did for Zechariah and Elizabeth. God did what seemed impossible! No one could believe Elizabeth and Zechariah could have a baby at their age.

Word spread across the whole country about God's miracle. People thought for sure John would grow up to be someone special because his birth had been a miracle.

And that's exactly what happened. John grew up to tell lots and lots of people about Jesus.

Bible Study

The story of Zechariah and Elizabeth reminds us that God can turn impossible situations into possible ones. God reveals his mighty power in situations that seem impossible for humans to solve or work out.

Is there something going on in your life right now that seems impossible to fix or change? Never doubt that God can use his power to change an impossible situation. God is so powerful that he can do anything he wants to do. Nothing is too hard for God. Nothing is out of reach for God's mighty power.

Talk to God. Tell him your problems and concerns. Each day, pray about what's going on. Keep talking to God often about your needs and worries. It took a long time for Elizabeth to finally have a child, but when the time was just right, God gave Zechariah and Elizabeth a son.

Sometimes you may feel like God doesn't hear your prayers. But that's not true. God hears every single one of your prayers. He even hears the ones inside your head and heart that you don't say out loud. God is always working on your behalf.

God can make the impossible happen. He did it for Zechariah and Elizabeth, and he can do it for you. Never stop praying. God never stops listening. He wants what is best for you. He loves you that much!

Reflection

- Has there ever been a time in your life when something felt impossible? How did God help you in that impossible situation?
- When have you had a task that felt too hard to accomplish on your own? Did you talk to God about that? God doesn't expect us to do everything on our own. Many times, we'll need to rely on his strength to get the hardest things done.
- When Zechariah couldn't speak, he had a lot of quiet time with God. The season of Advent is a good opportunity to spend extra time with God, away from all the noise and busyness of the holidays. Have you had quiet time with God today?
- Why is it important to spend time with God every day?

Prayer

Dear God, I'm so glad nothing is impossible for you. When I face a challenge that seems impossible, help me remember to talk to you. Please give me peace to know you always hear my prayers and you always work for my best interest. Remind me often of your mighty power. Remind me that nothing is too hard for you, God. Even when it seems like my prayers aren't answered right away, help me remember to keep praying. Amen.

DECEMBER 6

John Prepares the Way for Jesus

LUKE 1:67–80, 3:1–22; MATTHEW 3:1–17; JOHN 1:1–28

It probably doesn't surprise you to know that John ended up being a pretty special person. When God performs a miracle and sends an angel to deliver the news, you know what's going on is important.

God also gave Zechariah the words of a promise to speak over John. John would be a prophet—he would actually be the *last* prophet, because he was born just a short time before Jesus was born. Elizabeth, John's mom, and Mary, Jesus' mom, were relatives! So John and Jesus were cousins!

God used one final prophet to spread the news that the Messiah was coming. They didn't have social media and television that could announce the big news, so God used people who would travel to all the cities and towns speaking to the crowds. That's what John did.

When John grew to be a man, he wasn't like most people. He lived in the wilderness and ate bugs and honey and anything he could find in the desert. He wore clothes made of camel hair. He lived a simple life, but his words were powerful!

John's job was to "make a way" for Jesus and tell the people that Jesus would save them from their sins. He wanted people to prepare their hearts for Jesus. That meant people should look into their own hearts and feel sorry for the times when they'd hurt others. Jesus wants us all to have clean hearts and that starts with feeling sorry for our bad choices.

John told the people to stop sinning and "repent," which means to turn away from sin.

John took people into the Jordan River to baptize them. To baptize someone means using water to symbolize the washing away of sins so their soul can be sparkly clean. John told them being baptized would help them remember to stop sinning and to do what was right. That's how he got the name John the Baptist.

John's role in helping the world know about Jesus was predicted by a prophet named Isaiah. Isaiah lived long before John was ever born. But he said one day God would send someone who would make a way for Jesus and he would be like "a voice of one calling in the wilderness."

Isaiah's prophecy about John came true.

Zechariah's prophecy about John came true.

When God has a plan, that plan always comes true. God wanted Isaiah and Zechariah to tell others about John, and that's just what happened. God wanted John to tell people to prepare their hearts for Jesus. When you have a special visitor coming to your house, your mom or dad probably tells you to go clean your room. You might even have to take a bath, brush your hair, and use a toothbrush! All that preparation is so when the special person arrives, you'll be at your best for them. John did this for the people so they'd be prepared when Jesus arrived.

The people asked John how God wanted them to live. "What should we do?" the crowd asked.

John told them to share their blessings with others. He told them to take care of other people by giving them clothes if they need clothes to wear and food if they need something to eat.

He told the tax collectors not to charge more money than they should. He didn't want them to take money that didn't belong to them.

John the Baptist told the soldiers to treat people fairly and not accuse others of things they didn't do.

Some of the leaders thought John might be the Messiah—the one God promised to send to take away the sins of the world.

"No, I'm not the Messiah," John told them. "But he is coming soon."

Many people came to John to be baptized. Some came from places close by and some traveled a long way to hear John speak and to be baptized. And one of those people was Jesus himself!

As a human adult, Jesus came to John at the Jordan River and asked John to baptize him. At first, John said he wasn't worthy to baptize Jesus. "You should be baptizing me," John said.

But Jesus insisted. He told John it was part of God's plan. Baptism is a symbol of washing away sins and starting a new life. Even though Jesus never sinned, his baptism was a sign of his obedience and dedication to his Heavenly Father.

Jesus wanted to teach us to submit to God and be baptized as a sign of our dedication to Jesus as God's one and only Son. When we accept Jesus as our savior, we become part of God's family—that makes us all brothers and sisters!

Jesus and John stepped into the cool water. John held onto Jesus' shoulders and leaned him back into the water. As soon as Jesus was baptized, heaven opened. The Spirit of God, in the form of a dove, came from heaven, and a voice said, "You are my Son, whom I love; with you I am well pleased."

John told the people, "Jesus is the Lamb of God, who takes away the sins of the world. This is the man I told you about when I said, 'One is coming after me who is much greater than me. I baptize with water, but he will baptize with the Holy Spirit.'"

John told crowds of people, "Jesus is God's chosen One."

Bible Study

When other things crowd our hearts and minds—things like sin or a bad attitude or an idol that isn't God—then we don't have room in our heart for Jesus. An idol can be anything that we allow to become more important in our lives than Jesus—like watching television, gaming, playing sports, hanging out with friends, or shopping for expensive clothes or toys.

When we let one of those idols take up too much of our time or our thoughts, we don't have time or room for Jesus.

John the Baptist encouraged others to turn away from sin and prepare their hearts for Jesus. He wanted them to make room in their hearts for the Savior, God's one and only Son.

Are your heart and mind cluttered with so many things that you don't have room for Jesus? Advent season is the perfect time to prepare your heart for Jesus. Clean out things in your mind and heart that take the place of Jesus.

Leave plenty of room for Jesus in your heart. Prepare your heart for Jesus during Advent. You'll be so glad you did, because Jesus is the best gift you can receive this Christmas.

Reflection

- What do you need to do to prepare your heart for Jesus? What changes can you make to create more room in your heart and mind for Jesus?
- Is there a sin in your life that you're struggling to overcome? Ask Jesus and the Holy Spirit to help you avoid that sin. With the Holy Spirit's help, what can you do to help you break that sinful habit?
- John told everyone to turn away from their sin and repent. He wanted every person to prepare their heart for Jesus. Who can you tell about Jesus? Is there someone at school or baseball or dance that needs to hear about Jesus?
- Why do you think John wanted to live a simple life, without fancy clothes and food and a place to live?

Prayer

Dear God, show me what I need to do to prepare my heart for Jesus. As I count down the days of Advent and the arrival of Jesus, help me get rid of sin in my life. Help me clear away the clutter that fills my heart and mind. Show me how to make room in my heart for the very best gift of all—Jesus. Thank you for the promise of your Son. Thank you for Jesus. Amen.

DECEMBER 7

God's Plan for Mary and Joseph

MATTHEW 1:1–2:23; LUKE 1:26–38, 2:4–5, 3:23–38

God carefully picked out Jesus' earthly mom and dad, because he knew it would take special people to raise his one and only Son to be the Savior of the world.

The Bible doesn't tell us a lot about Mary and Joseph. Some of the things we believe to be true about them come from what we generally know about people who lived during that time. And people who have studied the Bible for years and years have shared facts they've learned about the time period when Jesus was born. Other information about Mary and Joseph comes from what we know about God.

By reading God's Word, the Bible, we can know more about God's character and trust he would have picked good parents for Jesus. God would have chosen loving, kind, and patient people. He certainly would have looked for two people who would love Jesus with their whole hearts.

And God would have chosen a couple who had a strong relationship with him, who worshiped and served him. God most certainly would have chosen a man and woman of integrity and good character.

That's exactly why God chose Mary and Joseph to be Jesus' mother and father. God had big plans for Mary and Joseph. Being Jesus' parents was a special, hugely important job.

From Bible verses in the Old Testament that foretold Jesus' birth—that means the verses talked about his birth a long, long time before he was born—people knew God planned for Jesus to be born to a family from the tribe of Judah. That was one of the reasons God chose Joseph to be the earthly father of Jesus, because Joseph's family was part of the tribe of Judah.

Joseph worked as a carpenter. Most carpenters back then led simple, humble lives. They weren't rich or fancy people. God chose a humble carpenter to be the earthly father of Jesus. He knew Joseph would love Jesus just like his own son and take good care of him.

By the time we learn about Mary in the Bible, she is already engaged to Joseph. The Bible calls it "betrothed." That means Mary and Joseph agreed to get married once a period of time had passed, which for them was a year. We don't really use that word much today. Being betrothed in those days was more of a binding, serious agreement than most engagements today. And the only way to end a betrothal was to get an official divorce.

Mary was very young, probably fourteen or fifteen, when she became a mother for the first time. She was a kind, humble, gentle girl. She lived a simple life and loved her family members. Though she was a good person, she wasn't perfect and needed Jesus to be her Savior too. Mary loved the Lord with her whole heart.

At the time, neither Mary nor Joseph was rich or famous or royal. They were not popular among the people nor were they important leaders in their community. People living back then might have said they were just ordinary people.

Yet God chose these two ordinary people to do a really extra-big, extraordinary, magnificent, special job—to be the earthly parents of the Savior of the world, Jesus! Mary and Joseph trusted in God's plan for their lives.

Bible Study

You can trust God's plan for your life too. Maybe you're feeling like God wants you to do something special this Christmas season. You might have thought of a special project you can do around the house to help your parents.

Maybe there's a neighbor who needs a little extra help this Christmas season. Perhaps you've had an idea to be kind to someone at church who doesn't seem to have a lot of friends.

Maybe God wants you to be brave and volunteer for a special job at church or school.

The Advent season is a great time to do something special for someone in your family, in your neighborhood, in your school, or even your community. Any time is a great time to serve the Lord, but the Christmas season is a perfect time to show the love of Jesus to others.

If you feel God tugging on your heart to do something big this Advent season, follow through on those feelings. Do what you feel like God is leading you to do, and trust God's plan for your life. That's important to remember always, not just during Advent.

You don't have to wait until you're older to do something big for God. He may very well have plans for you to do something big now. And maybe something even bigger next year or the next or several years from now.

Be prepared for how God can use you. Keep your mind and heart open to God's leading. He has big plans for you!

Reflection

- What special gifts and talents do you feel that God has given you? How do you think God wants you to use those gifts to honor him and to bless other people?
- Why do you think God chose Joseph to be the earthly father of Jesus? What character traits do you think he had that helped God choose him to be Jesus' dad?
- Why do you think Mary was God's choice to be the mother of Jesus? What character traits do you think Mary had that made her the perfect choice to be a good mommy for Jesus?
- How can you serve God even as a young person? What are some things you hope to do for God as you get older?

Prayer

Dear God, I know you have big plans for me. Help me be open to whatever you have planned. Prepare my heart and my mind to do the jobs you have planned for me. I want to love you with my whole heart. Help me learn more and more about you each day so I can tell others about Jesus. Help me be good and kind. I love you, God. Amen.

DECEMBER 8

An Angel Visits Mary

LUKE 1:26–38

When God decided the time was just right to send his Son to earth, God sent the angel Gabriel to Nazareth. God told Gabriel the words he wanted the angel to say to Mary.

Mary might have been sweeping the floor or baking bread. Perhaps she was taking care of her family's animals or doing some other chores. And then suddenly, an angel appeared and surprised her.

"Do not be afraid, Mary," the angel Gabriel said. But of course, she probably was just a little frightened at first. After all, she'd never seen an angel before!

"Greetings, Mary," the angel said next. "You are highly favored. The Lord is with you."

Most likely, Mary was stunned to hear these words from the angel. Mary, a humble, kind young woman, was not used to someone saying she was highly favored. She didn't have a wealthy family. She wasn't special or important. She was just an ordinary Jewish girl.

Gabriel gently told her again not to be afraid. He said, "Mary, you have found favor with God. You will conceive and give birth to a son, and you are to call him Jesus."

Mary listened closely to every word the angel said.

"Your son will be great," Gabriel told Mary. "He will be called the Son of the Most High."

Mary probably couldn't believe her ears! She probably couldn't believe that God had chosen her—an ordinary young girl—to be the mother of God's Son. God must have thought she was special if he chose her to raise his Son.

Gabriel continued to talk to Mary: "The Lord God will give him the throne of his father [ancestor] David." He told her Jesus would be King forever. His kingdom would never ever end.

Mary carefully listened and believed every word the angel said. She knew the angel spoke words from God.

But she didn't understand how she could be the mom of a baby boy.

"How can this happen?" she asked since she was not married yet.

Even though Mary was betrothed to Joseph—remember, that means they were engaged with a very serious agreement to get married after about a year—Joseph was not her husband just yet. She and Joseph were not married. She couldn't understand how she could be pregnant with a baby boy.

The angel explained it to Mary. "The Holy Spirit will come on you, and the power of the Most High will overshadow you." He told her the baby born would be "called the Son of God."

To remind Mary that God can do the impossible, that God can do anything, the angel told Mary that her relative, Elizabeth, was going to have a child. Everyone knew that Elizabeth had never had a child and was too old to have a baby.

Gabriel said, "Even Elizabeth your relative is going to have a child in her old age." God's words and promises always come true.

Mary treasured these words from the angel. She knew she wasn't super important. She knew she hadn't done anything special to earn God's favor. In other words, Mary realized that God's grace and favor were free gifts that couldn't be earned. In other words, Mary didn't deserve God's grace because of who she was or what she'd done. Mary received God's grace as a free gift from him because he loved her that much. And he does the same for us.

Mary was grateful for God's favor and grace. She was happy God had chosen her to be the mother of his Son. Mary said to the angel, "I am the Lord's servant. May your word to me be fulfilled." That means she wanted the words the angel said to come true.

And with that, the angel left.

Mary probably thought about Gabriel's words for a long time after he left. Because Mary loved the Lord and had worshiped him her whole life, she knew that he had promised a long, long time ago to send someone to be the Savior of the world.

Mary's parents or maybe her cousin Elizabeth might have taught her that the prophet Isaiah said that a young girl who has never been married will have a son. He will be called Immanuel, which means "God is with us." She probably remembered the prophet Isaiah also said, "The Lord comes with power, and he rules with a mighty arm . . . He tends his flock like a shepherd: He gathers the lambs in his arms and carries them close to his heart; he gently leads those that have young."

Someone must've taught Mary when she was a little girl these words from the prophet Daniel, written long before Mary was born: *All the nations will serve and obey God's Son.*

Mary probably knew all about God's plan to send a Savior. She most likely knew the prophets' words about the Messiah that would come one day. But Mary had no idea she would be the blessed one to deliver the baby boy who would grow up to save the world.

Mary might have pondered Gabriel's greeting. Gabriel's words in the Greek language meant something like this: "Rejoice because you have been given grace." It reminded Mary that she didn't earn God's grace nor had she done anything to deserve God's grace. Mary knew God gave it to her because he wanted to. Because he loved her that much. Because he is a God of grace and mercy who forgives humans of their sins.

The world had waited a long time for God to fulfill his promise to send a Savior. And Mary was part of that big plan. "Jesus is coming soon," Mary pondered quietly.

Bible Study

God offers grace to each one of us. We can't earn God's grace. We can never be good enough to earn God's grace. God gives us grace just because he loves us—not because we deserve it. He loves us so much he keeps giving us grace and more grace and even more grace.

The Bible is full of stories about people who did not deserve God's grace. Those people—like us—made many mistakes and bad choices. We sin and we turn our backs on God. We forget to praise him and thank him. We don't deserve God's grace and good gifts.

But God also knows we can never be perfect. God knew the world needed Jesus to take away our sins. When we trust in Jesus as God's Son, our sins are forgiven. If we trust Jesus as our Savior, one day, we'll spend eternity with God in heaven.

We should never take God's gift of grace and forgiveness lightly. God loves us so very much that he chose to send his only Son to earth to save us from our sins. God's grace—his favor he gives us in big ways—is never-ending, just like his love for us.

The Bible tells us his mercies are new each day. That means the love he has for us and the care he gives us are never-ending. His forgiveness of our sins, over and over, has no end.

God's grace, mercy, forgiveness, and LOVE never end.

Reflection

- How do you think you would have reacted if an angel surprised you with a message from God? Do you think you would have been scared?
- Mary knew about God because her family members taught her about him. She didn't have a Bible like we have today. Priests taught the people about God from words written on paper called scrolls. Families also memorized many of the Scriptures so they could pass down the Word of God through the generations. Aren't you glad we have a Bible to read today?
- How can you learn more and more about God? Do you read your Bible every day? Why do you think it's important to read God's Word often?
- How can you show God how much you appreciate his grace and mercy and love? What words can you say to him in thanksgiving?

Prayer

Dear God, thank you for the Bible, from which I can learn more about you. I'm so grateful for the grace that you give me, even though I don't deserve your favor. Thank you for showing me your grace every day. I'm grateful for the good gifts you give me. You are so good, God. You are holy and perfect and good, and I'm so grateful. Thank you for Jesus. I love you, God. Amen.

DECEMBER 9

Mary Checks In with Elizabeth

LUKE 1:39–56

Soon after the angel Gabriel visited Mary to tell her she would be the mother of God's Son, Mary took a trip to see her cousin Elizabeth. When Gabriel told Mary she was to be the mother of Jesus, he also told her that Elizabeth, her relative, was pregnant in her old age.

The Bible doesn't tell us why Mary traveled to see her cousin for certain. But we can figure out some of the reasons why.

Mary knew her cousin Elizabeth was too old to have a baby under normal circumstances. Mary knew Elizabeth's baby was a miracle given to her by God. Mary believed the words the angel told her about Elizabeth. She had faith that the words from God were true. And Mary was so excited that her cousin was finally going to have the baby she'd dreamed of and wanted for a long time!

Mary most likely wanted to go to Elizabeth to celebrate the new baby Elizabeth was carrying in her womb. Mary also probably wanted to help Elizabeth during her pregnancy. And quite possibly, Mary wanted to tell Elizabeth in person what the angel had told her about Mary being the mother of Jesus.

If anybody could understand the miracle of Mary being pregnant, it was most certainly Elizabeth. Both women were carrying miracle babies! Elizabeth and Mary were expecting special gifts from God!

Elizabeth lived in the hill country of Judea. That was about ninety miles from Mary's home in Nazareth. The journey from Mary's home to Elizabeth's home would have taken Mary about four days or more if she traveled by donkey.

The Bible doesn't tell us exactly how Mary got to Elizabeth's home or if she went alone or with others. It would have been very unusual, and unsafe, for a young woman to travel alone. Mary trusted God to take care of her on the journey. She had great faith in God to always be with her and never leave her, no matter where she traveled.

When Mary arrived at Elizabeth's home, she announced her arrival.

The moment Elizabeth heard Mary's greeting, she felt the baby in her womb leap for joy. The Bible says, "Elizabeth was filled with the Holy Spirit." That must've been quite a treat for Elizabeth to feel her baby respond to Mary's greeting in such a special way. She knew there was something special about Mary at that moment.

According to the words we read in this passage about the two women, Elizabeth knew about baby Jesus before Mary told her. The Holy Spirit helped Elizabeth know that Mary was pregnant with God's Son.

Elizabeth said, "Blessed are you among women. And blessed is the child you will bear!"

Elizabeth also said, "Blessed is she who has believed that the Lord would fulfill his promises to her!"

Mary did believe God. She believed God's promise that she would be the mother of the Son of God. She believed God would send a Savior to take away the sins of the world, and she had faith God would honor his promise to her to deliver baby Jesus into the world.

Mary had a strong faith. Because God chose her to be the mother of Jesus, we can figure out that Mary trusted God for a long time. But her faith in God grew even stronger as she trusted him to fulfill his promise to send Jesus to the world through her.

Mary used her words to praise God for what he'd done for her. The Bible calls it "Mary's Song." In the song Mary shares how happy and honored she feels to have been chosen by God to be the mother of Jesus.

Mary's words to God showed her gratefulness. Her words showed her strong faith in God. She trusted God to carry out his plans. She knew that God would keep his promise to her.

Mary stayed with her cousin for about three months. The women probably enjoyed celebrating their pregnancies together. Mary most likely took good care of Elizabeth while she was there. Mary could've helped Elizabeth do chores and get ready for her new baby boy, John.

We don't know for sure if Mary stayed until baby John was born. Perhaps she helped Elizabeth deliver the baby and then went home. Or maybe she traveled back to Nazareth before John arrived.

However the timing worked out, it's most likely true that the two women worshiped God and praised him often while they were together. Elizabeth praised God for her son, John, and for Mary's baby to come—Jesus. Mary praised God for choosing her to be the mother of Jesus and for her cousin's baby too.

Elizabeth and Mary were excited about baby Jesus coming soon. The season of Advent is a good time to let our hearts get excited about baby Jesus' arrival too!

Bible Study

Mary and Elizabeth celebrated while the babies grew inside their tummies. Both women knew the birth of the baby Mary was carrying would be the fulfillment of God's promise from long, long ago—the promise to send the world a Savior. Mary and Elizabeth knew they needed a Savior too. They longed for the baby's arrival and for the baby to grow into the man who would take away the sins of the world.

The women might not have understood exactly what that meant. They didn't have any idea that saving us from our sins would one day mean Jesus would have to die on a cross. They didn't understand all of God's plan, but they had faith to trust God and to trust his plan.

Mary and Elizabeth trusted God's plan for their own lives. They trusted God's plan for baby Jesus. And they trusted his plan for the whole world.

You can trust God's plan for your life too. God has a plan for every person. And because we know God is always, always good, we can trust that his plan for our life is good too. We can trust God. He will never leave us. He will never fail us. He will fulfill his promises.

God is always with us. He will never stop loving us. God wants us to put our faith and trust in Jesus as Savior of our lives so that we can live with him in heaven one day.

That's God's plan for us. That's God's plan for Jesus. God's plans are good.

Reflection

- God proves himself trustworthy to us over and over again. How has God showed you he can be trusted to take care of you?
- What makes it easy for you to trust God? When is it hard for you to trust God? What might help you trust God even more?
- Mary celebrated her good gift from God with words of praise that she shared aloud in a song. How do you celebrate the goodness of God? When recently have you celebrated something special God did for you?
- Think about the words you would say to God to worship and praise him. Write them down somewhere and then "sing" them back to God like Mary did.

Prayer

Dear God, help me trust you with a big, strong faith just like Mary. When something in my life seems hard, help me trust you even more in those times. When you give me good gifts and special favor, help me celebrate your goodness in big ways. Help me remember to tell others about the good things you do for me. Help my faith grow stronger and stronger every day, God. Thank you for taking care of me. Amen.

DECEMBER 10

Another Angel Visit

MATTHEW 1:18–25

When Joseph found out Mary was expecting a child, he didn't understand the baby was God's Son. Because Mary and Joseph weren't married yet, it was frowned upon for Mary to be pregnant. In fact, in those days, a woman and man could get in a lot of trouble if they were not married and were expecting a child.

Joseph loved Mary very much. He was a kind, compassionate man who loved God. He didn't want Mary to get in big trouble. He thought the best way to take care of this difficult situation was to divorce her.

He didn't want to cast a lot of attention on Mary right then, because he feared it might cause her to lose her life. The law said she could be stoned to death because of the unborn baby!

Joseph loved her too much to let anything bad happen to her. He thought a quiet divorce was the best answer.

Mary loved Joseph very much too. After all, they planned to marry at the end of their time of betrothal. Remember, a betrothal was like an engagement but taken much more seriously back then. It was a legal agreement that meant they would get married one year later.

Joseph tried hard to think through the situation and come up with the right thing to do. He was a devout Jewish man and loved God. And he also loved Mary. Joseph wanted to do what was right according to God. He wanted to obey the law too. And he especially wanted to treat Mary with kindness and love.

Before anything else could happen, an angel appeared to Joseph in a dream.

If you're remembering other Advent stories during this Christmas season, you'll remember that two angel visits had recently taken place. First, the angel Gabriel appeared to Zechariah to tell him about the upcoming birth of his son, John.

Zechariah doubted the angel. He didn't believe what God said. God extended grace and forgiveness to Zechariah for his lack of faith. But God punished him too. Zechariah couldn't talk until after the baby was born. Zechariah learned an important lesson about trusting God. He learned that God can do the impossible.

Six months after the angel appeared to Zechariah, Gabriel appeared to Mary. Gabriel told Mary she would be the mother of God's Son. Unlike Zechariah, Mary believed every word the angel said. Mary trusted God and never doubted his words. She had faith to believe God would do everything he said he would do.

Mary trusted God's plan for her. She knew God's plan was good.

In Bible days, God sometimes sent angels to give very important messages to people. Sometimes the Bible tells us the name of the angel. Sometimes the Bible doesn't mention a name.

God sent Gabriel to visit Zechariah and later to visit Mary. But the Bible doesn't mention the name of the angel that visited Joseph. It could have been Gabriel, but it might have been another angel. We don't know why God chose not to tell us which angel visited Joseph.

When we read God's words in the Bible, we can trust that he included the words he wanted us to read. Learning the truth in God's Word helps us know God better. It gives us the faith to trust God's promises. Knowing God's Word helps us trust God even more. Knowing God's Word is important. God's Word shows us how to obey him.

Joseph knew about the prophecies from long ago. Joseph knew God's promise to send a Savior one day. Joseph trusted God to fulfill his promises.

In Joseph's dream, God's angel said something like this: "Do not be afraid to marry Mary. The baby inside her is from the Holy Spirit. Mary will give birth to a son. You will name him Jesus because he will save his people from their sins."

The angel reminded Joseph in the dream about the prophecy from a long time ago, spoken by the prophet Isaiah. Isaiah had told the people that a girl who has never been married will give birth to a son. They will call him Immanuel.

When Joseph woke up, he knew God had spoken to him through the angel. Joseph trusted God. Joseph also loved God deeply and wanted to be obedient to him.

Joseph married Mary, just like God told him to do. Joseph trusted God's plan for his life. Joseph knew it would be a big job to be the earthly father of God's Son, Jesus. He knew this was a huge responsibility. He wanted to obey God and be the best father to Jesus he could be.

Mary and Joseph got good news from God about the baby that would join their family before long. Just like many people back then, Mary and Joseph had looked forward to a Savior for a long time. God's people had waited for the promised Messiah for years and years. Generations and generations of people who loved God anxiously waited for God's Son to be born.

The time was getting closer.

The Advent of the Savior of the world drew near.

Jesus was coming soon to change the world.

Are you eager to see Jesus?

Bible Study

Ever since Adam and Eve made a bad choice and sinned against God, the world has needed a Savior. We cannot save ourselves from our sins and wrongdoings. Only the perfect Son of God can save us from our sins.

God had a plan from the beginning of time to send his Son, Jesus, at just the perfect moment to be the Savior of the world.

Adam and Eve looked forward to the coming of the Savior of the world.

Abraham longed for the Savior.

Isaac, Jacob, and Judah knew a Savior was coming one day.

Tamar, Rahab, Boaz, and Ruth anxiously waited for the King of Kings.

David, Solomon—son of David and the third and last king—and their descendants awaited God's Son.

Zechariah and Elizabeth put their hope in God's promise and looked for the arrival of God's chosen Son.

Mary and Joseph couldn't wait to meet God's Son, the Savior of the world. They wouldn't have to wait long before baby Jesus would enter the world. Are you counting down the days till Jesus' birth?

While Mary and Joseph waited for their earthly son—God's holy and perfect Son—to arrive, they trusted God and his plans for their life. Mary and Joseph worked hard to obey God. The couple knew it was the right thing to do to obey God. They knew God wanted them to make right choices and obey.

Joseph knew obeying God showed his faith and trust in God.

Reflection

- How does reading and knowing God's Word help you obey God? What does it mean to you to obey God?
- Think about the last time you disobeyed your parent or your teacher. What were the consequences of your action? How did it make you feel when you were disobedient?
- What character traits do you think Joseph had that made him a good choice to be Jesus' earthly dad? What kinds of things do you think Joseph did with Jesus that made their relationship special?
- How do you think Joseph felt to be raising God's Son? Do you think Joseph made mistakes as a dad? How do you think he handled those mistakes? What do you think he did to fix his mistakes?

Prayer

Dear God, sometimes it's hard to be obedient. Help me know how to obey my parents and my teachers and other adults in my life. Please show me how to love you more and more, God. Help me obey you even when I don't always understand. Thank you for loving me so much that you sent Jesus to take away my sins. Thank you for always being with me. I love you, God. Amen.

DECEMBER 11

Mary and Joseph's Journey to Bethlehem

LUKE 2:1–5

A Roman emperor named Caesar Augustus was in charge of a large portion of the land around Mary and Joseph's country. He appointed a king, Herod the Great, to rule the area.

Herod the Great wasn't popular with the Jewish people. The Romans weren't popular with the Jewish people either. They changed too many rules for the Jewish people and didn't want them to worship God the way they knew they should.

Often, they collected more taxes than they should have from the Jewish people. Many of the tax laws were not fair to them.

Before Jesus was born, Caesar Augustus decided to take a census of the people. That means he wanted to count all the people in the land the Romans occupied. He made an announcement—a decree.

People had to travel back to the land where they grew up because Caesar Augustus thought this would be the best way to count everyone. The people had to do what the government ordered.

Each family made preparations for their trip.

Mary and Joseph lived in Nazareth. They had to travel to Bethlehem to be counted because that's where Joseph's ancestors were from. Think back to Jesus' lineage—his family tree—and you'll remember that Joseph belonged to the family of King David in Bethlehem.

The Bible doesn't tell us much about their trip, but we know several things because of maps and studying history.

Nazareth and Bethlehem are about ninety-five miles apart. To drive that far today in a car, it would take about two hours. But back then, with no cars yet and only rough walking paths, it would have taken Mary and Joseph about four days to get there. Maybe even longer since Mary was pregnant.

A few small towns and villages existed between Nazareth and Bethlehem back then. Maybe the couple found a home to spend the night in when it got dark, but they also might have just slept on the ground along the way.

Mary and Joseph loved the Lord. They knew God never ever left them. They knew God took care of them wherever they were, whether it was at home in Nazareth or on a rough and rocky road.

God watched over them at night while they camped beside the road next to a small fire to stay warm.

He watched over them on the first day of the trip. The second day of travel. The third and fourth and fifth day. God never sleeps—he took care of them every step of the way.

They knew God never left them, from Nazareth all the way to Bethlehem.

It was a difficult journey to say the least! Keep in mind there were no smartphones, no restaurants, no bathrooms, and probably very few snacks along the way.

Some of the land was rocky and unlevel. Sometimes the couple had to climb a hill or mountain. At times the vegetation was thick and thorny. Water was not always easy to find.

Not to mention the wild animals. Mary and Joseph had to be on the lookout for lions, bears, wild oxen, and maybe even a leopard or two!

Hunger. Thirst. Exhaustion. Sore legs. Hurting muscles. Maybe even bug bites!

Don't you wonder how many times Mary asked, "Are we there yet?"

Mary also might have been thinking, *Is it time for the baby yet?* The world had waited such a long time for a Savior. The people of the world knew they needed saving from sin and evil. But they also knew they couldn't do it on their own.

They needed God's Son, Jesus. Advent is the perfect season to think about how much you need a Savior. God sent his Son, Jesus, to the world for every person in the world. God wants everyone to know and love Jesus.

God knew we needed someone to save us. He knew it would be too hard for us on our own. We can't do this without Jesus. God's perfect Son, Jesus Christ, came to earth as a baby and grew up to be a man. One day, he died on the cross to save us from our sins. He took the sins of the world upon himself and took the blame for every person's sins. He took away the punishment for our sins so that we could be forgiven. If we love Jesus and accept him as our Savior, we can live eternally with God in heaven.

But Mary and Joseph didn't know all of those things would happen to Jesus when he grew up. Right now, they just knew he was coming to the world to save them. To save us. To save everyone.

They couldn't wait to meet baby Jesus, the Savior of the world. They knew he was coming soon.

Bible Study

Sometimes, life seems like it's working out just perfectly, with no problems or challenges. Our days and weeks just rock along, and life seems easy.

During those times, we can thank God for his goodness and grace and mercy. We should thank him for taking care of us and for all his good gifts. We should tell God often how grateful we are that he never ever leaves. We can thank him for always being with us.

Most of the time, however, life isn't that easy. Many times during the day or week, we face challenges and difficulties. Life seems hard and stressful. Problems come up that we have to solve. Things happen that we can't understand, and it's hard to find answers.

Life is just hard sometimes.

But you know what?

During those times, we can thank God for his goodness and grace and mercy. We should thank him for taking care of us and for all his good gifts. We can thank him for always being with us.

In good times and in hard times, God never ever ever leaves us. He never stops loving us. He is right by our side, giving us grace and mercy and strength. We can lean into his strength when we are too weak to keep going. And we can celebrate his goodness when life feels easy.

Just like Mary and Joseph, we can hang onto our hope in Jesus! He'll never let us down.

Reflection

- Think about a recent time when something really good happened to you. Did you feel God was with you during that time? Did you remember to thank God for that situation? It's never too late—thank him now!
- Think about a recent time that was really hard. Maybe when something didn't go quite right for you. Did you feel God's presence then? What did it feel like? Did you remember to thank God for being with you?
- How do you know God's with you in the tough times and in the good times? What helps you know for sure that God never leaves you?
- Do you know someone going through a difficult time right now? What can you do for that person to share the love of Jesus with them?

Prayer

Dear God, just like Mary and Joseph's difficult journey, life isn't always going to be easy. Remind me you're always with me, whether my journey seems easy or feels really hard. Thank you for always taking care of me and never leaving me. Help me put my hope and trust in Jesus. Please help me notice when others are having a tough time so I can lend a helping hand to those in need. Amen.

DECEMBER 12

No Room for Jesus

LUKE 2:6–7

Mary and Joseph finally arrived in Bethlehem. We don't know the details of their trip, but we know they made it to the town of Joseph's lineage so he could be counted. Remember—the word "lineage" means the people in your family that lived before you, like your parents and grandparents and great-grandparents. The Roman government wanted to know how many people lived in the Roman Empire so they could tax them properly.

The Bible doesn't tell us how long Mary and Joseph stayed in Bethlehem, either.

In fact, we know very little about this part of the story. But perhaps those details aren't important. What *is* important is that Jesus is due to arrive in a very short time.

God had promised his people for years and years that he would send someone to save them when the time was just right.

God's timing is always perfect. He always has a plan. And his plans are always best.

God is sovereign. That's a big word that means because he is God and is the Creator of all things, he has the power and the ability to do anything he wants, whenever he wants. We don't always understand what God does and what God allows to happen. There are many things that we will never completely understand. But because we know God is sovereign and because we know God is always good and because we know God wants what's best for us, we don't have to understand everything that happens.

We can trust God.

God may show us answers and reveal his plan to us on occasion. But we won't always understand. And that's okay. Mary and Joseph didn't understand everything that was going on during that time. But they trusted their sovereign Lord. They trusted God's plan for their lives.

Here's what we do know about this part of Mary and Joseph's journey. They had trouble finding a place to spend the night.

In just one part of a sentence in Luke 2:7, the Bible tells us, "There was no guest room available for them." Another version of the Bible says it this way: "There was no room for them in the inn" (NASB).

Back in the Bible days, when people traveled from place to place, they might stay in an inn, which was like a hotel. Not like the hotels we stay in today. Most inns back then were not as fancy and didn't have as many rooms as hotels today. Some inns might have a stable behind the inn for the visitors to keep their animals at night.

Or the travelers might have stayed in a guest room of someone's home. Most of the people during Bible days took great pride in taking care of other people. Their attitude of hospitality pushed them to make room in their own home for other people, even if it made their home crowded for the night.

People who had extra money during those days might have a home with a guest room upstairs. They might have had enough money to have a stable in the back of the house where the animals slept at night.

The less wealthy people of the day might have a very small home with one big room where the family cooked, ate, slept, and lived. There might be another small room on one side of the main room that was called the guest room.

And guess what? On the other side of the main room was a small area where the animals slept at night. That's right! The people often brought their animals inside the home at night to keep them safe from wild animals or from being stolen. That part of the house had a dirt floor. Built into the floor was a small manger—a feeding box for the animals.

Included in the main room would be a bigger manger where a larger animal could stick its head to nibble on hay or straw.

The Bible doesn't tell us exactly where Mary and Joseph stayed in Bethlehem. Some Bible scholars believe Joseph may have had some relatives still living in Bethlehem, but lots of people had traveled to Bethlehem to get counted. It's understandable that guest rooms in homes or all the rooms in an inn would already be full.

Mary and Joseph may have slept in a stable with animals. They may have slept in a very crowded home with no guest room, right next to the animals.

Wherever Mary and Joseph slept the night Jesus was born, we know that Jesus came into the world in a very humble way. He slept in a manger. An animal's feeding trough. There was no other place for the baby Jesus to sleep. From humble beginnings to the greatest man who ever lived.

Come, baby Jesus. King of Kings and Lord of Lords. He is God's Son. He's the Savior of the world. He's the best gift anyone could ever receive at Christmas or any other time.

Bible Study

God is sovereign. He can do anything he wants, whenever he wants, and however he wants. God could have given Mary and Joseph a fancy place to sleep for baby Jesus' birth. He could have given Jesus a palace to sleep in soon after he was born. He could have turned Jesus' birth into a huge celebration with tons and tons of people taking part in the festivities.

God chose to introduce Jesus to the world in a very humble, lowly way. God gave Jesus ordinary parents and placed him in an animal's feeding trough. God wants people to know that Jesus came for everyone. The rich and poor, the young and old, the smart and not-so-smart, the educated and uneducated, the good and the sinful, the mighty and the weak, the popular and unpopular. God wants everyone to know Jesus. He is everyone's Savior.

No matter what your status is, no matter how much money your parents make, no matter where you go to school or the color of your skin, no matter what your family looks like, God wants you to know that you are loved and that Jesus came to earth for you. Jesus came to the world for everyone. For Jesus that night, there may have been no room—except an animal's feeding box—but the best thing you'll ever do, the best decision you'll ever make in your whole life, is to make room for Jesus in your heart.

Reflection

- Sometimes the Christmas season is a busy, hectic time with all the preparations and shopping and baking and wrapping. At times, we can get so busy with Christmas-y things that we actually forget about the real reason we celebrate Christmas. Does that happen in your family? Do you have any ideas for how you could change that?
- The season of Advent encourages us to slow down and make room for Jesus. To eagerly await his arrival. To recognize he's the Savior of the world. What can you do to slow down and focus on the birth of Jesus?
- What do you need to do to make room for Jesus in your heart? Is there something you could give up to make more room for Jesus?

Prayer

Dear God, Bethlehem was a busy, bustling place when Jesus was born. Sometimes we let the Christmas season get too busy for us too. Help me slow down and focus on Jesus. Keep my mind and heart on the birth of your Son. Remind me that Jesus came for everyone in the world. Thank you for sending your Son to earth to take away my sins. Help me love Jesus more every day. Amen.

DECEMBER 13

Whose Manger Did Mary Borrow?

GENESIS 1:1–31; LUKE 19:40; JOHN 10:11–16; REVELATION 4:11; HEBREWS 11:3; ROMANS 11:36

Cows. Donkeys. Sheep. Goats. Chickens. Dogs. Camels. Geese.

What animals do you think were present at the birth of Jesus?

No one really knows the answer to that question for sure. That's another part of the story of Jesus' birth that we don't have all the answers to. Most Bible scholars think some animals must've been present or nearby when Jesus was born. Why? Because the Bible says Mary laid the baby Jesus in a manger.

A manger is a feeding box—or trough—for animals. Since we know from God's Word that Mary placed Jesus in a manger, we believe at least some animals were nearby when Jesus was born.

Knowing which animals were there doesn't change the story of Jesus' birth, but it's fun to imagine what animals may have been present.

God's creations are spectacular. From the tiniest insect to the largest whale and from the smallest dandelion to the massive oak tree, God's animals and plants are magnificent. The mountains and oceans he created are sights to behold.

Everything in creation points to God. God's creations are an expression of his glory and majesty. From the highest skies to the deepest oceans. If you want to know how amazing God is, look at the mountains and oceans and fields of wildflowers. All of creation is God's work of art—including you!

King David, a long time ago, wrote a psalm (another word for a poem or song) that said even the heavens and the sky cry out that God is glorious. Even though the sky and the heavens and the rocks and sea and animals can't speak, their existence cries out in worship for the Creator, God (see Psalm 19:1–4).

God's creations don't have to use words to declare the glory of God. The sheer beauty and magnificence of his creations exhibit his power and might.

When God created the world, just before he created Adam and Eve, the Bible says, "And God saw that it was good." God knew we would enjoy his beautiful creations. He made the plants and animals and mountains and seas to magnify his glory most certainly, but he also gave us these creations as a treat for us. God likes to give us good gifts, and his creations are some of the best gifts we could get!

God often uses his creations to teach us lessons too. Several verses in the Bible refer to sheep and shepherds. Jesus is even described as the Good Shepherd. A shepherd spends so much time with his sheep that they know him by his voice. The shepherd protects the sheep and is even willing to fight a wolf or leopard who might come to steal a sheep for their dinner. Jesus is the Good Shepherd because he would lay down his life for us, his sheep. The more time we spend with him reading the Bible and praying, the better we learn his voice, just like a little lamb! (See John 10 if you want to read Jesus' exact words about this.)

Maybe the manger Mary used belonged to sheep? How fitting that Jesus might have spent his first night in a manger that gave life to sheep and later Jesus would grow to be a man who gives his life to us and for us, his "sheep" that he loves and cares for so tenderly.

What if the manger Mary borrowed belonged to a donkey?

Just before Jesus' time came to die on the cross to save us from our sins, Jesus made a grand entrance into Jerusalem. Jesus rode in on a donkey, and the people shouted, "Hosanna! Blessed is he who comes in the name of the Lord! Blessed is the king of Israel."

The people praised Jesus and worshiped him with their shouts of "Hosanna!"

Riding the donkey in a grand entrance was Jesus' way of showing the people that he was the King of Kings and that he came in peace. Rather than riding a horse, which was often used by battle leaders, Jesus rode a donkey, a symbol of peaceful times of working in the fields.

Jesus' bed of hay in a manger could have belonged to a sheep or donkey. Or maybe another animal.

Whose manger did Mary borrow? We don't really know.

It's certainly fun to ponder which animals might have used the manger Jesus slept in on his first night.

Bible Study

All of creation glorifies God. Because we know God loves his creations and thinks they are good, we should want to take care of God's creations. We can be kind to animals and care for God's vegetation.

God's people took good care of their animals in Bible days. The people brought their animals inside the house at night for their protection against wild animals and thieves. That's why there was a manger inside the house where Jesus might have been born. Or perhaps Jesus was born in an animal stable near a house full of people.

We're not sure of the exact location, but we are sure the people took good care of their animals, just as God would want them to. And we're sure that baby Jesus slept in a manger, because the Bible tells us.

And that's most definitely fitting because if animals really were there when Jesus was born, they probably found a way of their own to praise the newborn King of Kings and Savior.

We can let God's creations be reminders that point us to God. Each time we see a pretty flower or rainbow or tall mountain or sandy beach or beautiful bird or fluffy cat or slithering snake or creeping spider—any time we see one of

God's creations—we can use that as a reminder to glorify God and say, "Thank you, God. Your creations are good."

Reflection

- Which one of God's creations do you think is the most creative? How do plants and animals and other creations point you to God? Which one of God's creations gives you the most joy? Thank God for one of his creations today.
- How do God's creations show his great power? How do his creations display his wisdom?
- God gave humans the responsibility of taking care of his creations. How do you do your part to care for his creations?
- How do you think God feels when someone mistreats one of his creations? Or when humans litter or don't take care of plants and trees and animals and oceans and seas and hills?

Prayer

Dear God, sometimes it's fun to think about what animals might have been with Mary and Joseph the night Jesus was born. Thank you for all your magnificent creations! Please let each of your creations remind me of you and your goodness. Let all your creations point back to you and glorify your mighty name. Help me do my part to take care of this beautiful world you created. Amen.

DECEMBER 14

No Need to Fear

LUKE 2:8–20; GENESIS 21:8–21; DANIEL 10:8–19; LUKE 1:11–38, 2:8–20; MATTHEW 1:18–25

Mary and Joseph traveled a long time and arrived in Bethlehem—check.

After finding no room at the inn, they searched for a place to stay—check.

Mary and Joseph finally found somewhere to spend the night—check.

The only place to lay the newborn baby when he arrived was a manger—check.

Parents-to-be Mary and Joseph checked off all the boxes as they awaited the birth of their baby boy. Mary knew it was time for the baby to be born. She'd waited nine long months for the arrival of her precious son.

The world, as well, had waited a long, long time for the birth of the Savior, the one who would save the world from sin and death.

He's coming soon, Mary must have thought.

"Jesus is coming," Joseph might have said.

They waited with great anticipation for his birth. Excitement must've filled the air. They knew this baby was going to make a difference. God's Son, Jesus, would change the world forever.

Are you looking forward to Christmas Day, the birthday of baby Jesus?

Christmas Day is less than two weeks away. On Christmas Day, we celebrate Jesus' birthday. Just like Mary and Joseph, we can eagerly await the celebration of his birth with great excitement because we know Jesus is the best gift we could ever receive!

In our minds, we can think about opening the grandest gift ever on Christmas Day—the gift of Jesus! It's like we already know what's inside the present, and we know it's the best present we'll ever get. And every day, we can live with excitement because we know Jesus' birthday is almost here.

To save the birthday festivities for Christmas Day, we'll hold the Advent story of Jesus' birth until December 25. On that day, we'll celebrate in grand fashion the greatest gift the world has ever known!

As excited as Mary was to soon be giving birth to God's Son, she might possibly have been a little frightened too. For one reason, she'd never had a baby before, and she may not have known what to expect.

But she also may have wondered how she, a young and ordinary girl, would take care of the Savior of the world.

Like with Mary, sometimes things frighten us. But we don't have to be afraid, because Christ has come and he promises to never leave us.

Just after Jesus was born, an angel visited and spoke these words: "Do not fear." But the angel wasn't speaking to Mary and Joseph.

Here's what happened.

One night, in a field outside of Bethlehem, a group of shepherds stood watch, guarding their sheep from danger. Suddenly a bright light surrounded them, and an angel stood right in front of them.

The shepherds were terrified! Nothing like this had ever happened to them before. Never ever.

The shepherds must have been shaking in their sandals!

The angel spoke to the shepherds, saying, "Do not be afraid, for behold, I bring you good tidings of great joy which will be to all people."

The angel was telling the shepherds that they had good news to share about Jesus' birth, but first, the angel wanted the shepherds to know they did not need to feel scared. The angel knew that Jesus was coming to save the world. But the shepherds didn't know that yet.

Many times in the Bible, God's angels appeared to humans to give messages. And a lot of those times, the angel's first words were "Fear not."

God understands that we humans have fears. He knows that we sometimes worry about situations that have already happened or things that might happen.

We humans can be easily frightened. God knows that, so his angels in the Bible usually say "Do not be afraid" before they share their message.

As far back as the beginning of the Bible, back in Genesis 21, an angel says to a woman named Hagar, "Fear not" (NKJV). Hagar and her son were in the desert and weak from lack of water. An angel appeared to Hagar and encouraged her. And God showed her a well full of water.

Another time in the Old Testament of the Bible, God sent an angel to a man named Daniel. God had a message for Daniel about what would happen to his people.

The Bible says Daniel trembled in fear.

The angel said to Daniel, "Fear not. Peace be to you; be strong, yes, be strong."

God wanted Hagar and Daniel to be strong, but God knew they couldn't be strong on their own. God encouraged Hagar and Daniel to depend on God's strength, not their own.

In earlier Advent stories, we talked about an angel appearing both to Zechariah, the father of John the Baptist, and to Mary, the mother of Jesus. The angel Gabriel said to Zechariah, "Do not be afraid." And he said the exact same words to Mary.

And you'll also remember that when an angel appeared to Joseph, he said, "Do not be afraid to marry Mary."

Many other verses in the Bible remind us not to be afraid. If God put those words in the Bible over and over, it must mean those words are especially important. We do not have to be afraid, because Jesus Christ has come and he promised he would always be with us.

In Matthew 28:20, Jesus told his disciples, "I am with you always, even to the end of the age" (NLT). Jesus didn't mean that he would be with them forever in his physical form. Because once Jesus went back to heaven after his death on the cross, he couldn't be with the disciples. But Jesus explained he would be with them forever in the form of the Holy Spirit.

The Holy Spirit, the third member of the Trinity, lives inside our hearts when we trust in Christ as our Savior. With the Holy Spirit dwelling within us, we do not have to be afraid. Jesus made sure we could lean on him for our strength, because the Holy Spirit gives us strength. We can be strong and "fear not."

Bible Study

It's hard not to be afraid sometimes, right? Because of sin in the world, there are plenty of things that happen in our lives that might make us scared. Like when we see a creepy spider while we're playing on the swing set. Or when we hear about a hurricane or tornado or bad storm. Or when the news talks about a big fire burning out of control.

We can also get fearful before a big test at school. Or when we move to a new city and meet lots of people we don't know. Or just before a dance recital or soccer competition.

In this world, we're going to have moments when we feel scared or nervous. During those times, we can call on Jesus to be our strength and to calm our fears. We can depend on the Holy Spirit to help us stay calm. We can remind ourselves that Jesus promises never ever to leave us. Nothing can happen to us that God doesn't allow. God is always there.

We don't have to be afraid.

The world needed Jesus to take away sin and death. This world needs Jesus to calm our fears. We can trust Jesus' promise to be with us "to the end of the age." That means forever and ever, and he means it! It's a promise we can hold on to.

Look forward to the birth of Jesus on Christmas Day. Remember that his birth will change the world forever. Celebrate the Advent of his coming.

And fear not, child of God. Fear not!

Reflection

- What sorts of things scare you? When are you afraid? What is your biggest fear?
- God knows your fears. God knows *everything* about us—our thoughts, our words, and our actions. He wants to comfort us in our fears. What do you think and feel when you hear that God knows about your fears?
- What can you do when you're scared that will help you remember Jesus is always with you? Do you remember to pray when you get scared? Who besides Jesus can you talk to about your fears? Tell an adult you trust about your fears.
- With help from Mom or Dad, look up verses about fear and God's strength in the Bible. Write them on notecards to read when you are afraid.

Prayer

Dear God, sometimes things happen in this world that make me scared. But just like the angel told the shepherds, Hagar, Zechariah, Mary, Joseph, and others, remind me I don't have to be afraid. Help me remember Jesus is always with me. Help me lean on your strength when I'm scared or anxious. Help me trust you when I'm nervous. God, help me "fear not." Thank you for sending Jesus. I love you, God. Amen.

DECEMBER 15

Joy to the Whole Wide World

LUKE 2:8–20

Let's talk some more about the shepherds who were visited by an angel. We can use our imagination and picture what this might have looked like.

The shepherds were guarding their sheep in a field outside of Bethlehem, minding their own business. From a field to the north, two shepherds made their way down the dusty road, gently nudging their sheep toward flat land near a stream. Three more shepherds wandered in the same direction, coming from the east. To the west of the field, another group of shepherds walked briskly, urging the sheep to keep moving forward. And from the south, a handful of shepherds made their way to the gathering point.

The shepherds probably greeted one another and made small talk as they collected their sheep in the same field.

"How are your sheep?" someone might have asked.

"Did they graze well today?" another might have said.

"Anything interesting happen in your field today?"

The shepherds probably chit-chatted as the sheep settled in for the night. Back in the Bible days, shepherds usually moved around from field to field to let their sheep graze and fill their bellies with fresh grass.

At night, they would sometimes gather in the same field to help each other protect their sheep from wild animals on the prowl. Perhaps they took turns sleeping, so that someone was always watching the sheep.

The next morning, each shepherd and his sheep would go their own way to look for fresh places to graze. Because the sheep recognized the voice of their shepherd, the flocks seldom got mixed up. They followed the voice of their beloved shepherd.

It was a hard job, and sometimes a lonely one too. The shepherds were usually alone all day with the sheep until they gathered at night.

On that special night of Jesus' birth, the shepherds may have just met up in the field. Darkness settled over the land as sheep huddled together in the grass. Maybe one or two shepherds were asleep. Maybe one shepherd was quietly singing. Maybe two shepherds whispered together as they kept an eye on the flocks.

Then suddenly a glorious light lit up the entire night sky, almost like it was daytime again! The sleeping shepherds awoke with fear. The singing shepherd hushed. Two startled shepherds jumped up and backed away from the strange sight. Their knees quaked. Their hands shook.

The angel said, "Do not be afraid, for behold, I bring you good tidings of great joy which will be to all people."

The shepherds couldn't believe their ears. The shepherds might have thought, *A message from an angel? For us?*

They listened closely to the angel's words. Next, the angel said, "Today in the town of David a Savior has been born to you; he is the Messiah, the Lord.

"This will be the sign to you: You will find a baby wrapped in cloths and lying in a manger."

The shepherds were stunned! "The prophets spoke of a Savior," one shepherd could have whispered to another.

"He's finally here," another shepherd may have responded.

As soon as the angel finished talking, a lot more angels appeared. The Bible calls it a "great company"—that means a huge number. This group of angels, much like a choir of angels, praised God. They said, "Glory to God in the highest, and on earth peace, goodwill toward men."

Wow! What a grand message was given to these shepherds. It's the very best message of all—Jesus is here! The Savior of the world is born today.

But do you know why it seems odd that shepherds were the first to receive the message of Jesus' birth?

During the Bible days, the occupation of a shepherd was not considered to be a grand position. It was a very lowly job. It was a difficult, stinky job that many people looked down on. Though it wasn't kind, many people thought shepherds were unimportant and inferior.

The angel's appearance to the shepherds pointed out an important message from God: Jesus came to the world to save *all* people.

Everyone.

Every. Single. Person.

From the lowly shepherd to the mighty king.

From the important to the ordinary.

From the high society to the homeless.

From the wealthy to the poor.

From the grand to the mediocre.

Jesus came to bring great joy to *all people*.

From his humble birth that placed him in an animal's manger, Jesus came for all. Even though he is the Almighty God, Jesus came to earth in humility to prove to the world that he came to save all of humankind.

The Bible says in Luke 19:10, "For the Son of Man has come to seek and to save that which was lost" (NASB). Without a Savior, everyone in the world is lost—lost to sin. That means Jesus came for everyone, because God knew we needed someone to save us from our sins.

The Bible also says, "For God so loved the world that He gave His only begotten Son, that whoever believes in Him should not perish but have everlasting life" (NKJV). That's

John 3:16, the most famous line from the Bible. Look at these important words in this verse: "For God so loved *the world*." God loves the entire world! Jesus' birth brings joy to the whole wide world, just like the angels announced to the shepherds.

Also in this verse, it says, "*whoever* believes in Him should not perish but have everlasting life." Jesus extends his offer of salvation to everyone who believes in him, from the lowly shepherd to the mighty king and everyone in between.

God sent his angels first to a group of lowly shepherds to share in the joy of Jesus' birth. This event serves as a reminder that Jesus, the King of Kings, came in humility to save all people—*all* people.

Bible Study

Everyone in the world needs a Savior. Not just the poor. Not just the rich. Not just those in a valued and respected position. And not just those who serve in a position that some think of as unimportant or lowly.

The entire world needed a Savior then. The whole wide world needs Jesus now.

Just think how the shepherds must have felt! Surely they knew that other people thought they were unworthy, lowly citizens. God reminded the shepherds he didn't think of them as unworthy and lowly. God chose them to hear the good news first.

Can you just imagine how honored they must've felt to be chosen to hear the greatest news of all? It must've made them feel grand and special, right?

Jesus loves everyone the same. He doesn't rank us in order of importance. What's important to Jesus is that we make room in our hearts for him. That we accept him as Lord and Savior of our lives. That we believe God sent him to earth to die for our sins so that we could one day live in heaven forever with God.

Jesus extends this same great message to each one of us. He wants us to know that he thinks we are grand and special.

He came to this earth to save everyone, and that means you too. Won't you get excited about Jesus' birth, just like the shepherds? Enjoy good tidings of great joy!

Reflection

- Have you ever felt like you were not good enough? What made you feel that way? Talk to an adult you trust about your feelings. They've probably been through a similar situation and can help you feel better.
- Is there someone at school or church or in your neighborhood whom others treat as less than or beneath them? Have you thought about ways you can help that person feel valued and important?
- Jesus came in humility, even though he is God. We can do our part to make others feel valued and worthy. Memorize Matthew 6:25 to help you remember how valuable you are to God, and let it help you value and respect others. "Therefore I tell you, do not worry about your life, what you will eat or drink; or about your body, what you will wear. Is not life more than food, and the body more than clothes?"

- What does "joy" mean to you? How can you live each day in joy because of Jesus' birth?

Prayer

Dear God, thank you for loving this world so much that you sent your only Son to be our Savior. Thank you for loving me with such a big, ginormous love that you sent Jesus to save me from my sins and live in my heart forever through the Holy Spirit. Help me feel valued and loved by you. Remind me to treat others as valued and loved too. I'm so glad Jesus came for all. Amen.

DECEMBER 16

Marveling at the Manger

LUKE 2:9–20

The angels appeared to the shepherds, first just one angel making the most powerful and wonderful announcement ever. Then, a whole company of angels—that means a lot of them—praising God, saying, "Glory to God in the highest, and on earth peace, goodwill toward men."

After that, the Bible says the angels left the shepherds and went back to heaven. What a sight that must've been!

Even though the shepherds were most likely stunned by this message, they wasted no time in their search for baby Jesus. One shepherd said, "Let's go to Bethlehem and see this thing that has happened, which the Lord has told us about."

The shepherds had probably heard of God's promise to send a Savior. They'd heard stories passed down from their parents and grandparents and family members about God's plan. They knew God promised for generations and generations to send someone to save them.

To some, the shepherds may have been considered lowly citizens, but to God, they were the perfect people to receive the birth announcement. The shepherds believed every word the angel told them. Their trust in God and faith in his Word helped them believe and know that Jesus had come to earth.

The Bible says next that the shepherds "came with haste." "Haste" means extraordinary speed and movement with great purpose. It means to hurry times one hundred!

Perhaps one shepherd stayed behind to tend the sheep. Perhaps all the shepherds went quickly and trusted God to take care of the sheep while they were gone. We just know the shepherds hurried to Bethlehem.

The angel said, "A Savior is born—Christ the Lord."

The Greek word "Christ" means the same as the Hebrew word "Messiah." Both words mean "the anointed one." In Bible days, especially in the Old Testament time of the Bible, anointing someone with oil was a sign that God was setting that person apart for a very special job or purpose. The "anointed one"—Jesus Christ the Messiah—was God's chosen person to fulfill the purpose of Savior of the world. The baby Jesus would grow to be a man who would one day save his people from sin and death.

We describe Jesus as being Christ the Lord—God's Son. The King of Kings. Savior of the world. Holy and perfect. Part of the Trinity, along with God the Father and the Holy Spirit. Royalty.

Yet he came to earth as a humble baby.

The angel pointed out that the shepherds would find the baby wrapped in swaddling cloths. You might wonder how that would be a clue. After all—every newborn baby during Bible days was wrapped in swaddling cloths after birth. Swaddling cloths were strips of material wrapped around the baby to keep them warm and cozy, to make them feel snug and protected so they would sleep well and stay comfortable. Today's moms and dads often swaddle a baby with a special blanket made to fit tight and snug around the baby.

The angel's words about the cloths let the shepherds know that even though he was God in human form, royal and perfect, Jesus started his life on earth like other normal babies.

But unlike normal babies, Jesus slept in a manger. An animal's feeding trough.

God wanted Jesus to be set apart as the anointed, chosen one who would grow up to be the Savior of the world. But God also wanted Jesus to start his life in a lowly, humble way so no one would feel they weren't good enough to be saved by Jesus. Jesus came for ordinary people, those who don't have a lot of power. But he also came for the important and mighty.

The Bible tells us in Luke 2:16 that the shepherds "found Mary and Joseph, and the Babe lying in a manger" (NKJV).

Today most people give baby gifts to the parents of newborn babies. Maybe they did back in the Bible days too. But the shepherds arrived empty-handed. They went straight from the fields to the manger with just their hearts open to welcome the baby Jesus.

After the shepherds saw with their eyes what their ears heard from the angel, they left and told everyone they met about Jesus.

And you know what the Bible says about the people who heard the shepherds' words? It says they marveled at what the shepherds said. That means the people were filled with wonder about Jesus. They were amazed and astonished to hear the good news!

Eventually, the shepherds returned to the fields with their sheep. Filled with the joy of Jesus' birth, the shepherds glorified and praised God for sending Jesus to be the Savior of the world.

God—and Jesus—deserve our praise and adoration.

Many Bible verses remind us to glorify God in everything we do.

Revelation 4:11 says, "You are worthy, O Lord, to receive glory and honor and power" (NKJV).

Psalm 86:12 reminds us to give our adoration to God with these words: "I will praise You, O Lord my God, with all my heart, and I will glorify Your name forevermore" (NKJV).

Another verse in Psalms says this: "Oh, magnify the LORD with me, and let us exalt His name together." That verse is found in Psalm 34:3 (NKJV). "Exalt" is another word for glorify or praise. It also means to honor.

We can exalt God because of who he is—he is the God of the universe. He deserves our praise and adoration. And we should especially praise God for the gift of his Son, Jesus.

Do you marvel about Jesus? Are you filled with wonder about Jesus? Does it make your heart burst with happiness to know Jesus loves you with a never-ending love? Are you amazed at our awesome Savior, Jesus?

Jesus, the Savior of the world, deserves our praise and adoration.

Bible Study

The shepherds knew just what they had to do after they'd seen the baby Jesus. They couldn't keep this great news to themselves. The shepherds wanted everyone to know about the birth of the Savior. After all, the world had waited a long time to see God's promise come true. They'd believed God's Word when he said he would send someone to save the world from sin.

The shepherds "came with haste" to find baby Jesus, and once they found him, it seems like they went with haste to tell everyone they met about the new baby. They just couldn't contain their excitement.

Maybe their faces glowed with joy. Perhaps their eyes sparkled with happiness. Each shepherd probably smiled from ear to ear! Their words about Jesus brought sheer delight to each person they told. The Bible says that people marveled.

And after they told everyone they could find about Jesus, they went back to their job of tending sheep. But they couldn't stop praising God! The Bible says they glorified God and praised him.

Knowing about Jesus should have the same response in our lives. Because we know the good news about Jesus, the Savior of the world, our hearts should burst with so much joy that we want to tell everyone we meet about Jesus.

Because of the birth of Jesus, our hearts can swell with happiness and spill over with praise and adoration for the Savior of the world. God deserves to be exalted.

Reflection

- What do you find so amazing about Jesus? What do you get most excited about when you think of Jesus? Do others around you know how you feel about Jesus? Have you told the people you know about Jesus?
- What do you think the shepherds talked about on the way to find Jesus? What do you think they said on the way back to the field? How were the shepherds' lives different after seeing Jesus?
- Name one way your life is different because you know about Jesus. How has knowing Jesus changed your life for the better?
- How do you praise God? How do you show him your love? Can you think of other ways to exalt God?

Prayer

Dear God, I want to show the same joy for Jesus that the shepherds did. Please help me live each day full of praise and adoration for you, because you are an awesome God. Thank you so much, God, for sending Jesus to earth to save me from the sins of the world. Help me give Jesus my praise and adoration, because he is worthy of my devotion. I exalt you, Lord! Amen.

DECEMBER 17

Pondering All These Things

LUKE 2; JOHN 1:14

When the shepherds visited Mary and Joseph and baby Jesus, their excitement bubbled over, spilling into the tiny room occupied by two new parents, a small baby, and maybe an animal or two wondering who was sleeping in their manger.

Their praise and adoration over baby Jesus filled the birthplace of the Savior of the world.

Let's imagine what the conversation between the shepherds and Mary and Joseph might have sounded like:

"We were sitting in the grass, watching the sheep," said one shepherd. "Most of the sheep had settled down for the night."

"Except those troublemaker lambs," another shepherd might have said. "They wouldn't stop bleating and baaing, looking for their mama sheep."

"Get back to the good stuff," one shepherd said. "The stuff about the angel."

"We were sitting in the dark, when all of a sudden, a bright light lit up the whole countryside. And then, you're not going to believe this—well, you probably will . . . An angel appeared and said, 'Do not be afraid. I bring you good news that will cause great joy for all the people. Today in the town of David a Savior has been born to you; he is the Messiah, the Lord. This will be a sign to you: You will find a baby wrapped in cloths and lying in a manger.'"

Then another shepherd stretched his hands out really big and said, "And right after that, a whole bunch of angels showed up—too many to count—and they praised God."

One more shepherd interrupted and said, "Here's what they said: 'Glory to God in the highest heaven, and on earth peace to those on whom his favor rests.'"

"And we came with great haste to see the baby," the last shepherd said.

Mary quietly listened to every word the shepherds spoke. She snuggled baby Jesus close to her body as they retold the story, bit by bit, not leaving out anything. Mary maybe thought about the angel who visited her, nine months ago, to tell her she would be the mother of God's Son.

The angel Gabriel had said words like this to Mary back then: "You have found favor with God. You will conceive and give birth to a son, and you are to call him Jesus. He will be great and will be called the Son of the Most High." Mary listened intently to the shepherds. The Bible says, "Mary kept all these things and pondered them in her heart."

Mary may have pondered, like the time the angel first visited her, why God chose her to be the mother of his Son.

She may have remembered some of her family members teaching her the words of Psalm 23 that say, "The LORD is my shepherd." She wouldn't have missed the connection between the Lord being her shepherd and God first revealing the message of Jesus' birth to shepherds.

Mary probably thought about God's goodness and faithfulness to keep his promise. He told Mary nine months ago she would be the mother of the Savior of the world. And God kept his promise to her. Mary most certainly felt highly favored after the birth of Jesus.

Mary most likely marveled over the knowledge that her sweet, precious, newborn baby son was God in human form. There's a big word that means "God became human," and that word is "incarnate." Sometimes people speak of Jesus as the "incarnate Word of God." And that means he is fully God and fully man too.

John 1:14 says, "And the Word became flesh and dwelt among us, and we beheld His glory, the glory as of the only begotten of the Father, full of grace and truth" (NKJV). Another Bible version, the New Living Translation, says it this way: "So the Word became human and made his home among us. He was full of unfailing love and faithfulness. And we have seen his glory, the glory of the Father's one and only Son."

Mary knew what a treasure Jesus would be to the world. She must have suspected the world was changed forever that night.

All because of the little one she held close while he was awake and who slept in a manger on a bed of hay.

Mary couldn't have understood everything about God's plan for his Son, Jesus. She didn't know exactly what would happen as Jesus grew into a man and started his ministry on earth. But she trusted God.

We don't always understand what God is doing in our lives either, but we can always trust God. Always. He will never let us down, and he will never leave us. His plans for us are good. He wants what is best for us.

God said in Jeremiah 29:11, "For I know the thoughts that I think toward you . . . thoughts of peace and not of evil, to give you a future and a hope" (NKJV).

Mary knew Jesus was the extraordinary Son of God. She knew God had a divine purpose for his life. She knew he was God in human form. But she also knew Jesus was her tiny, helpless, newborn baby boy. A special Son for the whole wide world. And God gave her the job of raising him.

And Mary treasured all these things and thought about them a lot. She had every reason to treasure those thoughts.

Jesus had arrived. The Savior of the world lay sleeping in her arms, and she was grateful and honored to be the chosen mother of the incarnate God.

Bible Study

God doesn't always do things the way humans think he should. In fact, he probably rarely does things the way we think he will. But you know what? That's why he's God.

He's all-knowing and all-seeing. God is omnipresent—which means he is everywhere at the same time.

God is omniscient, which means he knows everything—past, present, and future. He knows our every thought and he knows what's in our hearts.

And God is omnipotent. That big word means he's all-powerful. There is nothing God can't do.

We won't always understand what God is doing. We can't understand all his ways because he is God and we're not. We will never understand everything fully about God, but we can keep learning more and more about him by talking to God in prayer and by studying his Word, the Bible. And even though we don't always understand his plans, we can trust him.

We can trust God completely.

We read in Isaiah 55:8–9, "'For My thoughts are not your thoughts, nor are your ways My ways,' says the LORD. 'For as the heavens are higher than the earth, so are My ways higher than your ways, and My thoughts than your thoughts'" (NKJV).

That's God's way of explaining that his plans and thoughts are different than ours. And his plans are always for our best. We can trust God. From Mary's story we can learn to trust God. And we're also encouraged to "treasure up and ponder" all the things we know about Jesus. Keeping Jesus first and foremost in our hearts is the best treasure we'll ever find!

Reflection

- If you could find any kind of treasure, what do you wish you could find? What would you do with that treasure? Would you share it with someone else? Would you keep it for yourself?
- Jesus Christ, the incarnate Son of God, is the greatest treasure you'll ever find. He wants to have a relationship with you. He wants you to ask him into your heart, to accept him as God's Son and the Savior of the world. Have you asked Jesus to be your Savior?
- How do you think Mary felt when a band of shepherds showed up at her door after she'd just given birth to Jesus?
- What sorts of things do you ponder about Jesus? What helps you trust Jesus?

Prayer

Dear God, please help me trust you more each day. Show me how to completely trust you, even when I don't understand your ways. Help me know you better. Give me a desire to draw closer to you through prayer time and Bible reading. Thank you for never leaving me. I'm thankful you're always with me. Thank you, Jesus, for coming to the world as the incarnate Word of God. I love you, Jesus. Amen.

DECEMBER 18

God Keeps His Promises

LUKE 2:22–38

Shortly after Jesus' birth, Mary and Joseph journeyed to the temple in Jerusalem to present baby Jesus to the Lord. They wanted to dedicate their firstborn son to God, just as Jewish rules and customs required. Back in those days, Jewish women presented sacrifices, like an offering, to God at the temple after giving birth to a baby.

Jewish law required Mary to offer a lamb as a sacrifice. But the law also said the couple could offer two doves or pigeons if they couldn't afford to buy a lamb for the offering.

Mary and Joseph didn't have enough money for a lamb. We know that because the Bible tells us they offered two turtledoves or pigeons. God chose a poor couple to be the parents of his Son, the Savior of the world.

God doesn't choose people to fulfill his purposes based on riches or wealth or prestige or status or education or skin color or popularity. God delights in choosing people who have a heart for him, a heart willing to serve and obey him.

Sometimes he chooses people to accomplish his will and purpose who we might question or wonder why he chose that person. God always knows best. God looks at the heart, not outside appearances, not material wealth, not previous accomplishments.

You may think you are too young or not smart enough or don't have enough money to make a difference for God. Don't let those things fool you or keep you from doing big things for God. Remember, Mary was a young, ordinary, poor girl, and look how God used her!

While Mary and Joseph were at the temple with baby Jesus, something really cool happened.

Let's back up just a bit. A man named Simeon lived during the time Jesus was born. In fact, Simeon was an old man by the time of Jesus' birth. Simeon was a good man who loved God and obeyed him. Simeon knew that God had promised to send a Savior. He believed God's promise.

The Holy Spirit revealed to Simeon that he would not die before he saw Jesus. Every day, Simeon waited for the birth of Jesus. He waited with expectation—he knew it would happen before he died.

Every day, Simeon wondered, *Will this be the day I see Jesus?* He kept his eyes open for the Savior of the world. He focused his heart and mind on the arrival of Jesus, God's promise.

On the day Mary and Joseph brought Jesus to the temple, Simeon felt a nudge from the Holy Spirit to go to the temple.

The very second he saw Mary and Joseph with the baby, he knew it was God's Son.

He might have thought, *This is the one. This is him. God's chosen one. God's promised Savior. The one who'll save the world from sin and death. The greatest man ever to be born. Fully God and fully man. The incarnate one—God in human form.*

He most likely could not contain his excitement and joy. Joy for Jesus.

Simeon took baby Jesus in his arms and praised God. Simeon told the Lord he could now die in peace because he had seen his salvation. He knew God sent Jesus to save all people.

Mary and Joseph marveled at Simeon's words. Sure, they'd already heard these words before, when the angel visited each of them. But they just couldn't help but get excited with every thought of Jesus saving the world.

One look at baby Jesus, and Simeon knew his hope had been fulfilled. In his arms, Simeon held the confident hope of God's answered promise—Jesus. Simeon knew salvation for all of humankind is found in the person of Jesus Christ.

And as if that wasn't enough excitement for Mary and Joseph that day, they also met Anna. A widow named Anna lived at the temple. She was only married about seven years before her husband died. From that point on, Anna lived at the temple serving and worshiping God.

The Bible says she prayed night and day, never leaving the temple. She waited a very long time for God to carry out his promise to redeem Israel. Remember, to "redeem" means to rescue or deliver. Israel needed to be redeemed from sin and its consequences.

She knew about the prophecies that foretold the birth of Jesus. She knew God would keep his promise to send a Savior. Her dedication to serving God through prayer and worship for years and years and years serves as a reminder to us.

Sometimes, we have to wait patiently for God's perfect timing for his plans to be revealed. While we're waiting, we can serve him through prayer and worship and dedication, just like Anna.

After years of waiting, Anna finally met baby Jesus. She'd waited and believed. Once she met Jesus in the temple, the Bible says she told everybody she knew that Jesus had arrived.

Simeon and Anna were different in a lot of ways. They had similarities too. Both Simeon and Anna were good people who loved God. They were just—which means they worked hard to do right—and they were sincere in their love for God.

Both anticipated the birth of Jesus with great passion. They knew all about God's Word and God's promises. They paid attention and learned Scripture from their family members and others.

Simeon and Anna kept their focus on God. Each day, they tuned their mind and heart to God. They thought about Jesus a lot. When would he come to earth? When would God send someone to save the world from sin and restore a right relationship with God?

Not only did Simeon and Anna know about God's promises, but they believed them too. They knew God would keep his promises.

Simeon's life was forever changed after he met Jesus.

Anna's life was forever changed after she met Jesus.

Jesus changes lives.

Bible Study

Simeon and Anna anticipated Jesus' birth. Every day, they hung onto hope that this might be the special day—the day of his arrival! They probably thought over and over, *Is Jesus coming today?* They kept their focus on Jesus, night and day. While they waited patiently, they served the Lord with worship, prayer, and devotion.

Advent is the perfect time to wait for baby Jesus with great expectation. Jesus' birthday is one week away. It's an exciting time to think about his arrival. We can focus on Jesus night and day too. We can know the Scriptures, like Simeon and Anna did. They didn't have a Bible like we do today. In their time, most of the Scriptures were memorized by family members who taught their children to memorize. Scriptures were also written down on lots of scrolls. Jewish people would attend synagogue to hear God's Word read aloud by the rabbi—another word for a teacher—who would also explain what the Scripture meant.

We are blessed with God's Word in the form of the Bible. We can read and know all about God from the Scriptures. We can learn more and more about Jesus when we read the Bible.

And we can serve God each day through worship and prayer. God desires a relationship with each one of his children.

He wants our attention. He wants us to focus on Jesus, to keep our hearts and minds on him.

God promised to send a Savior. God promised Simeon he would see Jesus. Anna believed God's promise to send Jesus. God kept his promise. God always keeps his promises. We can trust God to keep his promises.

Reflection

- Has someone ever made a promise to you they didn't keep? How did you feel when that happened?
- Have you ever made a promise you didn't keep? Did it bother you not to honor your promise?
- Sometimes people let us down. At times, we're the ones to disappoint someone by letting them down. God is the only one who will never ever let us down. God is dependable. We can trust God. He won't let us down, and he always, always keeps his promises.
- Have you ever waited a long time for something you wanted? Did you wait patiently like Simeon and Anna? Was it hard to wait? What did you do while you waited? Did you talk to God while you waited?

Prayer

Dear God, with Christmas just one week away, please help me keep my mind on Jesus and anticipate his arrival with great passion. It's easy to get caught up in other things happening during the holidays that take my attention away from Jesus. Show me how to keep Jesus in my heart night and day. Show me how to serve you with my prayers, my attention, and my devotion. Help me worship you and celebrate Jesus. Amen.

DECEMBER 19

Seeking Jesus

NUMBERS 24; MATTHEW 2:1–8

About the time of Jesus' birth in Bethlehem, wise men who lived far away noticed an unusual star in the night sky. The men recognized it as a sign of the birth of Jesus. They left almost immediately to seek the newborn king.

People who have studied the Bible believe these men may have come from as far away as southwest Asia, or maybe even farther. The men who traveled seeking Jesus were sometimes called "wise men," and sometimes called "magi," and sometimes called "kings." No one knows if they were actual kings, but they were smart men who studied a lot and may have been early scientists.

Bible scholars believe the men knew the star announced the birth of Jesus most likely because of the long-ago prophecy spoken by a man named Balaam.

In the book of Numbers in the Old Testament, a wild story that sounds like it's right out of the movies takes place. This was a long, long time before Jesus was born.

The king of Moab, whose name was Balak, was not a good guy, and one might be inspired to call him the villain of the story. He didn't like God's people, the Israelites, living near his country. The Israelites were on their way to the Promised Land. They hadn't made it there yet, and because of their disobedience and lack of trust in God, they were wandering in the wilderness and camping out near the country of Moab.

This angered Balak. He sent for a sorcerer, a man named Balaam, because he wanted Balaam to come to his land to put a curse on God's people. Balak believed Balaam could use his words to make bad things happen to God's people.

Balaam didn't want to do the job, even though he didn't worship God. Balaam worshiped other idols and gods. But he told Balak he could only say what God allowed him to say.

And not only did he use his words to say good things about God and his people, he blessed the Israelites and he foretold Jesus' birth to all of the people of Moab, saying a star would rise in Israel!

Somehow the wise men far away in other countries knew about the prophecy of the great star. Years and years and years after Balaam made the prophecy, a new and brilliant star appeared in the heavens at night. Apparently, the wise men had been watching and waiting for the star to appear.

"It's here," one wise man might have said. "The bright star is here! The newborn king has arrived!"

The wise men knew it was the sign of Jesus' birth. They packed up and left shortly after seeing the star. They wanted to find Jesus.

While we don't know exactly how many wise men traveled to Israel, it is believed they were important, intelligent men who were kings or worked for kings, because they brought a lot of helpers and assistants with them.

Some believe as many as three hundred men traveled as a group to find Jesus.

The men knew their journey would take them to Israel. Other Bible prophecies from long ago helped them know where to go. Even though the wise men weren't followers of God, they knew about him from Scripture.

The entourage—which means a group of people traveling together—made their way to Jesus. They sought the newborn king.

When the wise men got to Jerusalem, their conversation may have sounded like this:

"Let's go see King Herod," said one wise man. "Surely he'll know where we can find the newborn king."

"Good plan," said another wise man. "A man as important as the king will know about this spectacular event."

Another wise man might have added, "Perhaps he saw the great star. I'm sure he's found the newborn king by now. He must be as excited as we are to find the miraculous one."

But Herod and all of Jerusalem were troubled by the news. They didn't like the idea of a "new king" taking the place of King Herod. They were jealous. And they didn't like the idea of someone else getting attention and worship.

Sadly, King Herod knew nothing about baby Jesus. He called in Jewish leaders and asked, "Where did God say the Christ would be born?"

When they told him prophecy spoke of Jesus' birth in Bethlehem, King Herod sent the wise men there to seek Jesus. He told them, "Go and search carefully for the young child, and when you have found him, bring back word to me, that I may come and worship him also."

But, just like villains in storybooks and on television, King Herod was lying. He didn't have any plans to worship Jesus. He wanted to know where he could find Jesus so he could eliminate him—get rid of him. King Herod didn't want competition.

Meanwhile, the wise men, anxious to seek Jesus, left to make their way to Bethlehem.

Can't you just hear the clomping of camels' feet—or maybe horses' feet—tromping all the way to Bethlehem with men who were seeking Jesus? It must've been a sight to see!

Bible Study

When the wise men finally saw the bright star sign in the sky, they couldn't wait to meet Jesus.

Do you eagerly look for Jesus? Do you seek him each day? Are you using this time of Advent to turn your heart toward Jesus and think about him often?

We can seek Jesus and draw close to God through our daily prayers. God wants to have a relationship with us, and we can do that through prayer. Give thanks to God in your prayers. Talk to God about your needs. Share your heart's desires with him too. He wants to hear from you.

We should seek Jesus daily with our thoughts and our actions too. When we ask Jesus into our hearts—when we tell him we want him to be Lord of our life—Jesus sends the Holy Spirit to reside within us. Jesus is with us, night and day.

Through the Holy Spirit, Jesus helps us make wise and good choices. The Holy Spirit helps us know right from wrong. The Holy Spirit helps us be kind to others and treat people with respect. The Holy Spirit helps us know Jesus better.

We can seek Jesus by reading God's Word, the Bible. The Bible teaches us about God and Jesus.

Praying, reading God's Word, and seeking Jesus every day with our thoughts and actions help us grow into a mature believer and a better person. In other words, doing these things makes us pretty *wise*. Seek Jesus like the wise men did.

Reflection

- How do you seek Jesus with your words each day? What about your actions at home and away from home? How does your life show those around you that you love God?
- How can you be sure to make time to seek Jesus with your prayers during the busy holiday season? How can you make sure not to get too caught up in the chaos of Christmas shopping and wrapping and baking and playing that you forget to talk to God each day?
- Why do you think King Herod was so jealous of baby Jesus?

Prayer

Dear God, please help me seek you with the focus and determination of the wise men. Help me look for you from the moment I wake up until the minute I fall asleep. Keep my thoughts on Jesus. Turn my heart toward the newborn king. Help my actions reflect my love for Jesus. Help me seek the Savior of the world from sunup until sundown. Help me love Jesus more and more each day. Amen.

DECEMBER 20

Exceedingly Great Joy

MATTHEW 2:9–12

Clip, clop. Clip, clop. Clip, clop. Remember all those camels' hooves headed toward the little town of Bethlehem? The camels—or maybe horses—carried wise men seeking Jesus.

The entourage of wise men and maybe their helpers had come from lands really far away, because they saw the brilliant star in the sky. They recognized it as a sign of Jesus' birth.

And now they were almost there! Soon, they would see Jesus!

Maybe along the way they talked about finding Jesus.

One wise man might have said, "I can't believe we get to see Jesus soon. I've waited such a long time to meet Jesus."

"What do you think he looks like?" another wise man might have asked.

"I bet he has dark eyes. And a head full of dark curly hair. That's my guess."

One man pondered aloud, "How will we know where to find him?"

"I think we'll know," someone answered. "The God of the universe brought us this far. I think he'll lead us the rest of the way too."

And that's exactly what God did. Matthew 2:9 says, "Behold, the star which they had seen in the East went before them, till it came and stood over where the young Child was" (NKJV).

Just like that, God gave the wise men another sign to find baby Jesus. The same star they'd seen back in their country led them to the house with Jesus. The Bible says, "When they saw the star, they rejoiced with exceedingly great joy."

Exceedingly. Great. Joy.

Read that again—*exceedingly great joy.*

That's how we should always feel about Jesus!

CLIP, CLOP. CLIP, CLOP. CLIP, CLOP. The wise men galloped even faster! Jesus was so close now, so very close.

The wise men must have jumped off their camels and practically run inside the house.

The Bible tells us what happened next. "And when they had come into the house, they saw the young Child with Mary His mother, and fell down and worshiped Him."

Don't miss that part either—it bears repeating! They worshiped him.

Jesus deserves our worship.

Maybe the wise men worshiped with song or music or dance. Maybe all three. The wise men may have worshiped him with words of praise. Perhaps they clapped their hands or shouted in joy. Maybe they lifted their hands high and shouted.

Maybe each wise man worshiped Jesus in a different way. They "fell down and worshiped" him. They knew he was holy and set apart to be the Savior of the world. God's Son, God's chosen one.

After they worshiped Jesus, the wise men presented the gifts they'd brought with them from far away. The Bible says, "They opened their treasures." The wise men brought the very best gifts they could find for Jesus. They knew he deserved their best.

Gold. Frankincense. Myrrh.

Special gifts for a special baby.

Gold represented a royal gift fit for a king. They knew from Scripture that Jesus would be called King of Kings. To show respect for this newborn king, the wise men brought gold.

Gold, a precious metal, was the perfect gift for the precious Son of God. It was considered a valuable metal then, just like now, so it was fitting to give such a gift to God's only Son.

Frankincense, a thick liquid substance with a strong, sweet smell, was another valuable gift. Priests used it in the temple as a base to make incense. They would then burn the incense as an offering to the Lord.

Myrrh, more valuable than gold during the time of Jesus' birth, was a dried gum that came from the balsam tree. Sometimes it was in liquid form and used as a fine spice. Myrrh was used as an ingredient in special mixtures the priests used for anointing.

Jewish people used myrrh like medicine sometimes. They often coated a dead person's body with myrrh to prepare the body for burial. The strong scent of myrrh helped hide the smell of a dead body. Myrrh, with its many uses, was considered a product of great worth.

Gold, frankincense, and myrrh. Treasured gifts of great worth for the greatest treasure of all—Jesus.

The wise men brought valuable, expensive gifts for baby Jesus, and they worshiped him. Yet the humble shepherds came to see Jesus with no gifts—just a heart ready to love him. And they worshiped him too.

God loves our gifts to him, but he treasures our worship even more. When we give him our heart and attention, that's what he loves most. He wants a relationship with us.

After the wise men presented their gifts, they left baby Jesus with the intention of going home. They knew King Herod wanted them to go back to Jerusalem with an update about baby Jesus.

However, God warned the wise men in a dream not to go back to King Herod. God knew King Herod wanted to harm baby Jesus. The wise men followed God's lead and went a different direction to get home. They avoided Jerusalem and King Herod.

The wise men looked for Jesus and found him. They rejoiced with exceedingly great joy and worshiped him. In the moment of seeing Jesus, their lives were changed forever. They would never be the same again.

That's how it should be when we meet Jesus. Once we know Jesus, we should be different. Our lives should look different. We're changed forever. It may mean our lives will take a different path, just like the wise men. We'll want to walk a path that will please God and make him happy by making right choices and being obedient to him.

When God leads, we follow. Just like the wise men.

Bible Study

Sometimes seeking and following Jesus is easy. Sometimes following him takes a lot of work and effort, like the wise men's long journey. Easy or difficult, following Jesus is the best journey we'll ever take. And it will always be worth it. Jesus is worth the journey.

We can trust God to lead us on the journey with Jesus. He will show us the way. Wherever he leads, we should be obedient and follow. We can trust that we are doing the right thing by following God.

When we give our whole heart to God, we'll want to give him valuable, worthy gifts, just like the wise men. Giving him our heart is the most valuable gift we'll ever give Jesus! Telling others about Jesus is a worthy gift to share with the King of Kings. Giving money to our church as part of our tithes and offerings is like giving Jesus a gift too.

Serving others in need is a great gift to share with Jesus. God loves when we take care of others, especially those who are struggling or having a difficult time.

Treating people the way Jesus treated others is one of the greatest gifts we can give. Being kind to others—even those who don't look or act the same as we do—makes God happy and most certainly brings a smile to Jesus' face. It may not be a gift wrapped in a box and tied with a bow, but kindness is one of the greatest treasures we can offer another person.

Reflection

- What part about seeking and following Jesus is easy for you? What part about following Jesus has been hard for you? What helps you remember the journey is worth it?
- Think about a time when you felt like God was leading you to do something or say something. Did you follow God's leading? How did you feel when that happened? What helps you trust God's leading?
- What's your favorite way to worship Jesus? How do you like to praise him best?
- Sometimes people talk about the Three Wise Men because of the three gifts mentioned in the Bible. Most likely, more than three men traveled to seek Jesus. Just for fun, name three gifts you'd like to give Jesus in the coming year.

Prayer

Dear God, the wise men showed their willingness to follow your lead, even though they didn't know you very well at the time. Help me follow your lead, God, for short journeys and long ones too. Help me follow you the rest of my life! I know it will be the best journey I ever take! Remind me that my life should look different when I find Jesus and obey him. Thank you for Jesus. Amen.

DECEMBER 21

And Jesus Grew

LUKE 2:39–52, 3:22, 4:14–22, 5:12–14, 5:17–26; MATTHEW 10:2–4

When Jesus was still a young boy, Joseph moved his family back to Nazareth. The Bible doesn't include a lot of information about Jesus when he was growing up. But we can't let the silence about his childhood years take away from their importance. Whatever happened during that time, God was using those days and years to prepare Jesus for his plans.

Luke 2:40 says, "And the Child grew and became strong in spirit, filled with wisdom; and the grace of God was upon Him" (NKJV). Jesus was a fine young man who obeyed God and his parents.

Mary and Joseph raised their family to love and worship God. Each year, the family traveled to Jerusalem to celebrate the Feast of the Passover. Jewish families celebrate Passover to remember all that God did when he rescued them from slavery in Egypt.

When Jesus was twelve years old, the family traveled to Jerusalem, like always. Usually, a large number of relatives traveled together. After several days in Jerusalem, the family started the journey home to Nazareth. The Bible says Jesus stayed behind in Jerusalem. Mary and Joseph thought Jesus was with another family in the group heading home, so they didn't realize he was missing until the end of a long day's travel.

Frightened, Mary and Joseph hurried back to Jerusalem to search for him. That took a day of travel. And then they spent a day looking for Jesus there.

Mary and Joseph finally found Jesus in the temple, talking with Jewish teachers. He listened carefully and asked questions. The teachers who'd heard Jesus' words were amazed at his wisdom and understanding of God.

Mary might have said something like, "Jesus, where were you? Your father and I have been looking for you for three days!"

"Did you not know that I must be about My Father's business?" Jesus said.

Jesus obeyed his parents and went home with them to Nazareth. Luke 2:52 adds these words to the story to let us know what a good son he was: "And Jesus increased in wisdom and in stature and in favor with God and man" (ESV).

Even though Jesus was God's Son—God in human form—he grew up like a normal boy. He went to school, did his chores, loved his family, memorized Scripture, and loved God. This was God's way of preparing Jesus for the plans he had for him.

When Jesus became an adult, he worked as a carpenter, like his earthly father, Joseph. Jesus did carpentry work until he was thirty years old. Then the time came for him to begin his ministry.

Jesus began teaching in the synagogues. He read aloud the Scripture that foretold his birth. Then he said to the teachers and people: "Today this Scripture is fulfilled in your hearing." He was telling the people that he was the one the Scriptures talked about. He was God's Son!

Jesus wanted them to know that God had sent him into the world to offer salvation. That if we trust in him, believe in him, and put our faith in him, we will be saved. We must turn away from our sins and obey God. Then we will have eternal life.

Many people believed in Jesus and put their trust in him. Some people doubted him and turned away.

Jesus taught people about God and told them about salvation. That was the job God had for Jesus on earth. That was God's plan—to send Jesus to save the world from sin and wickedness.

Jesus also had a healing ministry. Over the three years of his ministry on earth, he healed the sick and took care of many people.

Jesus gathered a group of men to be his disciples—his helpers on earth to carry out his ministry. Jesus picked twelve special disciples, whom he called apostles, to be his close, intimate helpers, but many more disciples followed him and learned from him.

These twelve apostles included Peter, James, John, Andrew, Nathanael, James, Judas, Jude, Matthew, Philip, Simon, and Thomas. Jesus didn't pick the richest men. He didn't pick the most popular men. He didn't pick men who were perfect and nice all the time.

Jesus picked ordinary people, like fishermen. Jesus wanted others to know that God can use anyone for his purposes.

Together with his disciples, Jesus traveled all over teaching, healing, and performing miracles.

Once while Jesus was speaking to a large group of Jewish men who were teachers of the law, several men brought a friend to Jesus to be healed. Their friend couldn't walk. The men carried him on a mat.

Many people crowded the place where Jesus spoke. Everybody wanted to hear Jesus!

The friends had an idea. The conversation may have gone something like this:

"Let's climb on the roof and lower him down," one of the friends might have suggested.

"That sounds a bit dangerous," another might have answered.

"We have to try. I know Jesus can heal our friend."

The men carefully climbed on top of the house, removed part of the roof, and lowered their friend to Jesus.

Everybody must have been shocked.

But they were even more amazed at what Jesus said. He said to the man, "Your sins are forgiven."

This angered the Jewish leaders. "No one can forgive sins but God," they said.

The Jewish leaders didn't believe that Jesus was God's Son.

Jesus next said to the man, "Get up and walk."

Immediately the man was healed. He stood up and walked away. In fact, he was so excited to be healed, he probably danced and ran too.

Jesus healed the blind, deaf, and diseased. He helped people with mental illness. He healed the sad, broken-hearted, and lonely. He raised some people who had died back to life.

He preached and taught. He loved and helped. He showed compassion to many. He taught people how to love others and be kind. He was gentle. He was a friend. He loved God and he loved all people.

He was the greatest man to ever live on earth.

Bible Study

Though we don't know a lot about Jesus' time as a young boy, we learn much about Jesus' young life from this one verse: "And Jesus increased in wisdom and in stature and in favor with God and man" (Luke 2:52, ESV).

Jesus grew up like a normal kid, except he never sinned. He loved God perfectly. He obeyed God's commands. He loved his parents and obeyed them. He showed respect to the adults around him. He treated his neighbor as himself.

Jesus was perfect.

The Bible is quiet about Jesus' young days, but God used that time to prepare him for his ministry. God could have had Jesus be born already knowing all those things, but he allowed Jesus to learn them as a young boy so he could have compassion for others. So he could understand everything we think and feel.

God prepares us for the plans he has for us too. Our responsibility is to grow in wisdom and stature and in favor with God and man too. That means we obey God and our parents. We listen to our teachers and leaders and treat others with kindness. And we stay open to God's plan for us.

God has a plan for each of us. He will prepare us for those plans. How exciting to see what God has planned for our lives!

Reflection

- Which one of Jesus' miracles that you've read about is your favorite? If Jesus visited you at your house today, what miracle would you ask for, for yourself or a family member? (Don't forget—you can ask Jesus for anything—any miracle you want—through prayer. And if that's part of God's plan, he'll answer your prayer. You can always talk to God about anything!)
- Who do you know who needs one of Jesus' miracles, like healing from a sickness or help with some other issue? How can you remember to pray for that person each day?
- In what ways do you think going to school and learning will help you with God's plan for you? How will that equip you—or prepare you—to do God's work later?

Prayer

Dear God, thank you for sending Jesus. Thank you for letting me learn about Jesus through the Bible. Help me treat other people with great kindness and compassion. Show me how to help those in need. Help me do my part to show the love of Jesus to everyone around me. Help me grow in wisdom, Lord, so that I might better serve you. Prepare me for the plans you have for me. Amen.

DECEMBER 22

Dying to Set Us Free

MATTHEW 26–28; MARK 14–16; LUKE 22–24; JOHN 16–21, 3:16

Today's Advent story is a hard one to tell. It's a very sad time in the life of Jesus. Yet it is the most powerful and important part of Jesus' time on earth.

When Jesus began his ministry, he knew it would end in a terrible death to take away the punishment for our sins. Jesus loved us so much that he was willing to die for us. And as hard as it was for God to watch that happen, God loved us with such an incredible love that he was willing to send his only Son to earth to die for us.

Here's how that sad story took place.

After three years of ministry, Jesus knew the time of his death was getting close. Many of the Jewish leaders didn't like the things Jesus said. They didn't believe he was God's Son. Some of their dislike came from jealousy. They wanted to follow rules and laws, but they had no compassion for God's people. They didn't love others like Jesus did.

Some of the chief priests and other leaders plotted and planned a way to trick people into believing Jesus was guilty of doing wrong. They wanted him arrested so they could kill him.

All this happened during the Feast of Passover.

Sadly, one of the apostles, a man named Judas, went to the priests secretly. He told them he would betray—which means turn against—Jesus. He agreed to help them find and arrest Jesus.

"What will you give me to deliver Jesus to you?" Judas asked.

"Thirty pieces of silver," they answered.

Later, Jesus celebrated the Passover meal with his twelve apostles. The meal later became known as the Last Supper.

After the meal, Jesus went to a garden to pray while the disciples stayed close. Jesus said to God, "Yet not as I will, but as you will." He knew he would die soon, and he wanted to obey God. When he finished praying, Judas came with some of the men who wanted to kill Jesus. He led the men to Jesus. The men had swords and clubs. They grabbed Jesus and arrested him. Jesus' disciples were so scared, they ran away. No one stayed with Jesus.

The chief priests took Jesus to court. Some people lied about Jesus and said bad things about him. The priests and leaders didn't believe he was the Son of God. They accused him of talking badly about God.

The men put chains on Jesus' hands and feet. They plotted a way to have him killed.

The next day, they took him to the governor, a man named Pontius Pilate.

"Are you the king of the Jews?" the governor asked.

"You have said so," Jesus answered him.

Pilate didn't really believe Jesus had done anything wrong. He wanted to set Jesus free. He thought of a plan he hoped would work. Every year during the Passover feast, the governor released one prisoner. The governor thought the people would ask for the release of Jesus. But the chief priests and elders tricked the people into asking for the release of a prisoner named Barabbas.

"Barabbas," the people yelled.

"Then what shall I do with Jesus who is called Christ?" he asked the people.

"Crucify him," the people shouted. They shouted louder and louder until Pilate gave in. He released the prisoner named Barabbas and demanded that Jesus be punished.

He still didn't believe Jesus was guilty, and he said to the people, "I am innocent of this man's blood."

The story gets even harder to hear. People did really mean things to Jesus. But Jesus took all of their punishment for our sins.

The men hit Jesus with a whip that had sharp edges. The men mocked Jesus—which means they made fun of him—by making a crown of long, sharp thorns. They pushed the crown onto his head, put a robe on him, and called him "King of the Jews." The thorns poked into Jesus' skin.

Next, they led him away to be crucified. That meant they planned to hang him on a cross by nailing his wrists and feet to the boards of the cross. During Bible days, people often used this cruel punishment for criminals and people who did bad things.

But Jesus was innocent. He never sinned. He was the perfect Son of God.

The Roman guards nailed Jesus to the cross and stood the cross on a hill near Jerusalem. Though it was afternoon, darkness covered the land. Soon, Jesus stopped breathing and died. At that very moment, a veil—like a curtain—in the temple ripped from top to bottom. A large earthquake shook the mountains.

Even some of the Roman guards said, "Truly this was the Son of God."

Not all Jewish leaders were hateful towards Jesus. When evening came, a man named Joseph, who was a member of the Jewish leadership, took Jesus' body from the cross, wrapped it in a clean linen cloth, and laid it inside a tomb. He rolled a stone against the door to seal the tomb closed.

In three days, some of the women who loved and cared for Jesus and his apostles went to the tomb.

And here comes the happy part of the story. The best miracle ever!

The stone was rolled away, and Jesus' body was not inside! An angel told the women, "Do not be afraid, for I know that you are looking for Jesus, who was crucified. He is not here; he has risen, just as he said."

Jesus rising from the dead is called the resurrection of Jesus.

The women ran to tell the apostles. Along the way, Jesus appeared to them. They fell at his feet and worshiped him. Soon, other followers found Jesus too.

Jesus spent a few weeks with his disciples. He told them he had to go back to heaven to be with God, but he promised to send them a helper.

Jesus told them he would send the Holy Spirit to live inside their hearts so they would never be alone.

"But very truly I tell you, it is for your good that I am going away. Unless I go away, the Advocate will not come to you; but if I go, I will send him to you." The Advocate is another name for the Holy Spirit.

"I will be with you always."

He told them the Holy Spirit "will glorify me because it is from me that he will receive what he will make known to you." When we accept Jesus as the savior, the Holy Spirit lives in our heart, and that's how we can feel Jesus' presence in our lives.

Soon Jesus returned to heaven to be with God forever. The hard, sad story about Jesus' death has a happy ending. The happiest ending of all, because his death paid the debt for our sins and his resurrection changed the world forever.

Bible Study

The death of Jesus on the cross is a very hard story to hear. Many people were cruel to Jesus, and he suffered a horrible death. Jesus was willing to do all of that just for us! He didn't deserve death, but he loves us so much that he gave his life to pay for our sins. He died on the cross so that we could have eternal life in heaven one day.

That's a big, *big ginormous love*! Nobody else can love you that much. Not even your mom and dad who love you with an incredible love can love you as much as Jesus does. Not even your grandmommy or granddaddy can love you that much, even though their love is enormous! Not even your best friend loves you as much as Jesus does.

The Bible says in John 3:16, "For God so loved the world that He gave His only begotten Son, that whoever believes in Him should not perish but have everlasting life" (NKJV). Another version says, "For God so loved the world that he gave his one and only Son, that whoever believes in him shall not perish but have eternal life."

Jesus loves you enough to give up his life on the cross. He wants to spend forever with you. He died on the cross so that you can live with him forever in heaven one day. If you believe in Jesus, trust him as your Savior, and ask him to forgive you of your sins, you can have Jesus' gift of salvation and eternal life.

Reflection

- What made Judas betray—or turn against—Jesus? The Bible tells us that Judas gave back the thirty pieces of silver. He was sad that he had turned against Jesus. He wished he had not betrayed Jesus.
- Jesus is always ready to listen. He will erase your sins when you ask for forgiveness. When you do something that you know hurts Jesus, what can you do to make it right?
- What are some things you can do to show Jesus how grateful you are for his gift of salvation? Have you thought about helping someone in need, like Jesus would? Can you be kind to others, like Jesus?

Prayer

Dear Jesus, I know you died on the cross for the world's sins. I know you died for my sins too. I'm sorry for the times I hurt you with my sins. Please forgive my sins, God. Thank you so much for the happy ending to the story. Thank you for raising Jesus from the dead. Thank you for sending the Holy Spirit to be our helper on earth. Thank you for never leaving me. Amen.

DECEMBER 23

Jesus Will Come Again

MATTHEW 24:26–31, 24:36–44, 25:13; LUKE 21:25–28, 21:34–36; JOHN 5:28–29, 6:39–40, 14:1–3; ACTS 1:10–11; 1 CORINTHIANS 15:51–52; PHILIPPIANS 3:20–21; HEBREWS 9:27–28; 1 THESSALONIANS 4:16–17, 5:1–3; TITUS 2:11–14; JAMES 5:7; 2 PETER 3:8–10; REVELATION 1:7–8, 3:11, 20:11–15; ROMANS 3:23, 5:8, 6:23, 8:1, 10:9

The good news of the cross is that Jesus did not stay dead in the tomb. Jesus rose from the grave. He conquered death!

After his resurrection, he told his disciples that he would come again. Jesus announced his second coming. The first time Jesus came to earth, he came as a newborn baby. The next time Jesus comes, he will come as the King of Kings and Lord of Lords. The Bible says he will come again to take his people to heaven to live with him forever.

Jesus explained his return by saying: "But of that day and hour no one knows, not even the angels of heaven, but My Father only." God has a plan. God is waiting patiently for as many people as possible to repent and come to accept Jesus.

Jesus assured people back then and assures us with his words in the Bible that he will return. It's a promise we can believe.

Jesus said in John 14:1, "Let not your heart be troubled; you believe in God, believe also in Me" (NKJV). Then he described how heaven is like a huge mansion with many rooms. Jesus said he was going to heaven so he could get our rooms ready and that he'd come back one day and take us back with him where we'd live together forever.

Jesus says when the time comes, angels with loud trumpets will announce his coming. He will come to earth on the clouds and gather all those who believe in him.

How amazing it will be to see Jesus coming on the clouds. We will live with God forever and ever. God promises no more tears or sadness or pain or illness. God's people will spend the rest of their lives worshiping him in heaven.

It might even be like a grand celebration and party that never ends! A party hosted by God where Jesus is the star of the show. What a marvelous time of rejoicing and celebrating.

When Jesus returns, God's plan of salvation will be complete. Those who believe in Jesus and have put their trust in him will live forever in a new, perfect world.

Jesus wants to spend eternity with you. The only way to live with Jesus forever is to accept his gift of salvation, to put your trust in Jesus, and to believe in him as God's Son.

God is a holy and perfect God. Our sins separate us from God. He cannot have sin near him. We needed a way to be reunited with God. Jesus is the way.

Bible Study

No one knows when Jesus will come back to earth. Jesus said this to his disciples in Matthew 24:36 when he told them that no one knows the day or hour of his second coming. Not even the angels in heaven. Not even he knows. Only the Father in heaven knows.

Jesus also told them in Matthew 24:44 to be alert and watch for his coming. Always be ready for his return.

Jesus wants everyone to know he will come again. We can get just as excited about his second coming as we do about his birthday every year. In fact, we can be more excited about the next time he comes, because that means we'll get to see him face-to-face and live with him forever.

It will be an even bigger celebration than Christmas!

As we anticipate the celebration of the birth of Jesus in just two days, we can be mindful of Jesus' return. Are you ready for his return? Have you trusted in Jesus and asked him to be your Savior and the Lord of your life?

Have you put your faith in Jesus and believed in him? Jesus wants to give you the free gift of salvation. When you trust in Jesus, he accepts you as his own and promises to never leave you.

When you believe in Jesus, he will return for you one day. That's a promise he made, and he always keeps his promises. You can have eternal life when you put your trust in Jesus.

Reflection

- Have you ever asked Jesus to come live in your heart forever and then put your trust in him? If you want to do that today, can you talk to Jesus about your decision? After you talk to Jesus, tell a parent or Sunday School teacher about your decision. It's the best decision you'll ever make!
- What excites you the most about Jesus' return? What can you do to "be ready"?
- How does it make you feel to know how much Jesus loves you? What can you do each day that will remind you of Jesus' big love?
- Is there a sin you struggle with? What can you do to change that bad habit or wrongdoing? How can you let Jesus help you make that change?

Prayer

Dear God, thank you for loving me so much that you sent Jesus to be my Redeemer. Help me show my gratitude for the love of Jesus by making good choices and turning away from sin. I'm sorry when I do wrong things that hurt you. Help me live a life that is pleasing to you. Thank you for the promise that Jesus will come again. Thank you for Jesus. I love you, God. Amen.

DECEMBER 24

Sharing the Good News

ACTS 8:26–40

Before Jesus went back to heaven, he gave his disciples instructions to wait patiently for his return. He also gave them directions on how to live.

Jesus said something like this: "Go and make disciples of all the nations. Tell them the good news about me. Make sure they know about God's plan for salvation. God's plan includes all people of every nation. I want everybody to know about my free gift of salvation."

He gave the disciples instructions to baptize those who believe in him. "Baptize them in the name of the Father and the Son and the Holy Spirt," Jesus said.

Jesus asked us to teach others to follow his commands and instruct them to love God first and to be kind to others.

Jesus added one more thing: "I am with you always."

The Bible calls those words Jesus spoke "The Great Commission." A commission is a command or instruction. It's the "great" commission because Jesus wants everyone to know about him.

After Jesus went back to heaven, his disciples told people about him at every opportunity. One person who told lots of people about Jesus was a man named Philip. One day, an angel told Philip to go south along the road from Jerusalem to Gaza. Philip listened to the angel and went right away.

As Philip walked, he saw a man riding in a chariot. The man was from Ethiopia, a faraway place. He served under the queen of the Ethiopians, Queen Candace, and he had lots of authority in the queen's household. In fact, he was in charge of all of her money and treasures.

He was a big deal!

This man from Ethiopia had journeyed to Jerusalem to worship God. He'd read about God in the Scriptures of the Old Testament, but he didn't know about Jesus. He wanted to know more.

Sitting in his chariot, the Ethiopian read from the book of Isaiah.

The Holy Spirit urged Philip to go near the chariot. When he got close, Philip could hear the man reading from the prophet Isaiah.

Philip asked the man, "Do you understand what you are reading?"

The man replied, "How can I unless someone guides me?" The man must've suspected Philip could help him. He asked Philip to join him in the chariot.

This might have been an odd sight to see back in the Bible days. The Ethiopian was most likely a rich man with fancy clothes. Philip was an ordinary man. He wasn't wearing expensive clothes. And he certainly didn't serve royalty like the Ethiopian did.

It might have looked odd, too, because the men looked so different. Their skin color was not the same, and they came from countries far, far apart. The men had more things different about them than the same.

But that didn't matter. Those things weren't important. What was important was sharing the good news of Jesus. The Ethiopian wanted to know about God. Philip had been one of the twelve apostles; he had walked with Jesus and learned at his feet. Philip knew just what to say to share the good news of Jesus with the man. And he was excited to tell him about Jesus.

About that time, the Ethiopian man noticed a pool of water along the road. "Can I be baptized?" he asked Philip.

"If you believe with all your heart, you can be baptized," Philip answered.

The man from Ethiopia said, "I believe that Jesus Christ is the Son of God." He probably had a really big smile on his face when he said those words.

The important man from Ethiopia commanded his driver to stop the chariot. Philip and the man walked to the water. Philip baptized the man in the name of the Father and of the Son and of the Holy Spirit.

The Ethiopian rejoiced and went on his way. He was part of God's family now, forever and ever.

Bible Study

Just like most of the stories of the Bible, we can learn a lot from the story of Philip and the Ethiopian. The story highlights the importance of sharing the gospel—that means the good news of Jesus Christ. Jesus wants everyone to know about him. Many people won't ever know about Jesus unless someone tells them.

When we have Jesus in our life, this good news should be so marvelous and special to us that it bubbles out of us, causing us to share it with everyone we meet!

Just think about what might have happened next with the Ethiopian. The Bible says he went away rejoicing. He probably told his chariot driver about Jesus. Maybe the driver even heard Philip's words too. Perhaps he became a believer of Jesus right on the spot too. We don't know, because the Bible doesn't tell us, but it quite possibly could have happened.

Surely the Ethiopian went home and told his family members about Jesus. He probably told other people in the queen's household. He may have even told Queen Candace about Jesus.

And if each person he told then told another person . . . and then that person told another person . . . just think how many people might have learned about Jesus because Philip obeyed Jesus' instructions to share the good news.

Jesus commands us to tell others about him. Maybe each person we tell will believe in Jesus. They most likely will "go away rejoicing," too, just like the man from Ethiopia.

Reflection

- How often do people talk to you about Jesus? Do you remember the first time you heard about Jesus or was that too long ago to remember?
- Do you "go away rejoicing" whenever someone talks to you about Jesus? If you do, woo-hoo—you have the right attitude! If you don't, talk with your parents or guardian about some ways to get more excited about Jesus.
- How many times have you had the chance to share the good news of Jesus with someone? How did that person respond? Were they excited to know about Jesus?
- Think about someone new you want to tell about Jesus. Make a point to talk to that person soon. You just might change that person's life forever with the good news of Jesus!

Prayer

Dear God, thank you for the good news of Jesus. Now that I have this news—the best news anyone will ever hear—help me to want to share it with others! Remind me not to keep the news of Jesus to myself. Fill my heart with excitement about Jesus so that I "go away rejoicing" every time I think about your Son. Thank you so much for Jesus. Help me love him more each day. Amen.

DECEMBER 25

Jesus Is Here—the Best Gift of All

LUKE 2:6–7; JOHN 3:16; ROMANS 6:23, 10:9; 2 CORINTHIANS 5:18–19

He's here! He's here! It's Jesus' special day.

Happy birthday to you.
Happy birthday to you.
Happy birthday, dear Jesus.
Happy birthday to you.

Isn't it a marvelous day? A day to celebrate the Savior of the world. A day to celebrate God's only Son. A celebration for the King of Kings and Lord of Lords.

Jesus, God in human form, was born on this day many, many years ago.

The Bible lets us know Jesus is on the way with words like this: "While they were in Bethlehem, it became time for Mary's baby to be born." Then, in Luke 2:7, the Bible says very simply, "And she brought forth her firstborn Son, and wrapped Him in swaddling cloths, and laid Him in a manger" (NKJV).

It might be just a few words to announce the birth of God's Son, but the miracle of his birth on earth is nothing short of magnificent.

Just picture this in your mind . . . Mary waited nine months for baby Jesus to grow inside her. Suddenly, she knew the baby was on its way.

She might have quietly said, "Joseph, it's time. Baby Jesus is coming."

Perhaps some of the older women close to where Mary was staying came to help her deliver the child. Joseph may have held her hand and put a cool cloth on her forehead to help her feel better. The women talked gently to her and took care of her.

Maybe cows mooed softly somewhere nearby, like they were singing a lullaby. Joseph and Mary's donkey, waiting in the stable, could have shuffled his feet back and forth in anticipation of the new arrival.

Camels and sheep and chickens might have felt the excitement in the air with God's Son on the way.

God's animal creations may have known something big and special was about to happen.

Mary could have whispered to the women, "This is God's Son." Joseph might have told some of the men in the village, "God's Son is coming."

And then, during the hush of the evening, while the rest of Bethlehem and the world went about their usual business, a small cry could be heard. A tiny cry announced the Savior's birth. Mary probably counted fingers and toes. Joseph breathed a sigh of relief and hugged Mary.

Mary quickly wrapped the baby in strips of linen so Jesus wouldn't be cold. She held him close to her heart and kissed his tiny head. Joseph gazed into the newborn's eyes. He might have even whispered, "I'll take good care of you, my son." Or at least he felt this in his heart.

Maybe they cried tears of joy. Perhaps they sang songs of praise. Their hearts swelled with love and happiness.

And surely they gave thanks to God for their bundle of joy, because they knew this special baby would change the world. They realized they were holding God's promise to the world in their arms. God's gift to humankind, wrapped in swaddling cloths. Wrapped up tight and snug, like a present. Like the very best gift anyone could ever receive.

Baby Jesus is God's extra-special gift to us. John 3:16 says, "For God so loved the world that He gave His only begotten Son, that whoever believes in Him should not perish but have everlasting life" (NKJV).

For God so loved the world . . .

God's love is big and mighty and powerful and never-ending. God's love is so huge he chose to send his only Son to the world, just for each one of us. Jesus came to live with us on earth because he wants us to live with him forever and ever.

What a special gift to us, wrapped up in swaddling cloths.

Jesus came to give us salvation. When we put our faith in him and believe in him, when we trust him and ask him to be our Savior, we can be saved. We receive the free gift of salvation from Jesus. Romans 10:9 tells us, "If you confess with your mouth the Lord Jesus and believe in your heart that God has raised Him from the dead, you will be saved" (NKJV).

When we accept Jesus and invite him to live in our heart forever, it's like opening the best gift we could ever receive—the gift of salvation and eternal life. Jesus made a way for us to be part of God's family forever.

Sin separates us from God, but Jesus reunites us with God. The Bible says Jesus reconciles us with God—that means he restores us and puts us back together with God. The Bible uses words like this in 2 Corinthians 5:18–19: "Now all things are of God, who has reconciled us to himself through Jesus Christ . . . not counting our sins against us."

Because of Jesus, when we ask him to forgive our sins, God doesn't count our sins against us. We are no longer separated from God. We are part of God's family—we are adopted into God's family when we trust in Jesus. We belong to God's family forever and ever, and no one can take that away from us.

Jesus came to earth to give us the gift of eternal life. The gift of God is eternal life in Christ Jesus our Lord.

God had a plan for Jesus to be the Savior of the world. He promised to send Jesus, way back during the time of Adam and

Eve. When God makes a promise, he can be trusted to keep that promise.

Many years later, the promise of a Savior came true in the birth of Jesus. Jesus came to earth to live with us to teach us about God and God's love for us. He told us God wanted us to live with him forever and offered us the gift of eternal life through salvation with him.

Christmas isn't just about trees and lights and candy and decorations and stockings and toys and new clothes and shopping and gifts. Christmas is about *the gift*. The gift of Jesus.

There's never been another Christmas gift as wonderful as Jesus. Nothing can ever be more important than Jesus.

Our gift is Jesus. Celebrate his love for you and treasure him as a precious gift. It's the best gift you'll ever receive.

Happy birthday, Jesus.

Merry Christmas.

Bible Study

What did your home look like earlier today? Did wrapping paper and ribbons litter the floor? Did scrunched up tissue paper and empty boxes fill the garbage can? Could you smell the delicious aroma of turkey or ham drifting from the stove? Was a large pan of dressing bubbling in the oven and gravy simmering on the stovetop?

Did you share your day and the frenzy of opening gifts with family and friends? Did you play with new toys outside on a snowy day or in the backyard in the sunshine? Did you nibble on too much chocolate and a host of snacks throughout the day?

As Christmas Day comes to a close, the holiday season is almost over for another year. Soon, all the sparkly decorations and twinkling lights will find their way to the attic or storage containers. You'll make room for treasured toys and new clothes on shelves and in the closet. And maybe you'll start dreaming of next Christmas, a whole year away.

When you close your eyes tonight, imagine the baby Jesus, wrapped in linen strips like a finely decorated present. Imagine carefully holding baby Jesus, just like Mary did. Hold him close to your heart, like a precious and valuable gift.

As Christmas fades for another year, be sure to keep Jesus in your mind and heart in the year to come. Keep him close. He loves you with an everlasting love, and he wants to be with you forever.

Reflection

- Think about the best gift you've ever received. What was that gift? What is your favorite gift you've opened this Christmas? Even as special as those gifts are, nothing can ever compare to the gift of Jesus. What can you do to help you remember that Jesus is the best gift you'll ever receive?
- What part of the Advent and Christmas story is your favorite? The shepherds? The wise men? The angel visits? The birth of Jesus?
- Do you have a friend at school or in the neighborhood who hasn't heard about Jesus' birth? Can you share what you've learned about Jesus' birth with them?
- What do you think Mary and Joseph talked about after the birth of Jesus? What words do you think they said to each other and to God?

Prayer

Dear God, thank you for the greatest gift of all—your Son, Jesus. Thank you for sending Jesus to earth. Thank you for a love so big that you sent your Son, Jesus. I'm so glad he came to teach us how to love you and how to love others. Help me keep Jesus in my heart and in my mind every day. Thank you, God, for Jesus. I love you, God. Amen.

ACKNOWLEDGMENTS

To the four J's who made us parents, Jeremy, Jenifer, Jeb Daniel, and Jessica: You are our greatest treasures, and we love you dearly! Thank you for making every Christmas a treasured memory in our hearts.

To our extra blessings, Adam and Dawson: Thank you for making our Christmas festivities even more fun.

To our sweet grandchildren, Benaiah, Maverick, and Danae: Thank you for making Christmas—and every holiday—extra sweet!

To extended family, Lavenders and Blands: Thank you for fond Christmas memories over the years.

To dear friends we've celebrated with at Christmas and throughout the year: We treasure our memories of fun times together.

To our agent, Cyle Young: Thanks for everything!

To Penguin Random House: A huge thank you for another project we've enjoyed immeasurably. We're incredibly thankful for this opportunity and for every person who helped this book become reality. You're amazing!

Lastly, but first in our lives, to our Heavenly Father: We've tasted and seen—*you are good*!

ABOUT THE AUTHORS

Julie and David Lavender love old traditions of Christmases past and new adventures of Christmas present. Julie adores one particular family tradition—gingerbread house creating—so much that she recently published a children's picture book called *A Gingerbread House*. They love searching for Christmas trees on Julie's childhood farmland, climbing trees to snitch mistletoe, sipping hot chocolate after driving around town to look for Christmas lights, creating gingerbread villages and keeping them out all year long, wearing matching Christmas pajamas, and retelling the Christmas story with props on Christmas Eve.

With three grandchildren now, Julie and David especially love watching Christmas unfold and anticipating the birthday of Jesus through the eyes of little ones.

Julie, a former public school teacher and homeschooling mommy, has a master's degree in early childhood education. David, a former medical entomologist for the US Navy and wildlife biologist for an army installation, has a master's degree in entomology and a biology undergraduate degree.

Julie and David's six favorite humans are their adult children, Jeremy, Jenifer, Jeb Daniel, and Jessica, and sons-in-law, Adam and Dawson. And their most favorite people in the whole wide world are their three grandchildren: Benaiah, Maverick, and Danae.

Since David retired in 2024, Julie and David enjoy more time with their children and grandchildren, spend hours outdoors observing God's beautiful creations, and find lots of time to write together. They are the authors of books, magazine and newspaper articles, and devotions.

Their most favorite hats to wear? Mommy and Grandmommy, Daddy and Granddaddy.

ABOUT THE ILLUSTRATOR

Shahar Kober is an illustrator working from a very small studio, in a very small town, in a very small country. Over the years, Shahar has illustrated tens of books, but he also creates illustrations for newspapers, magazines, and animated films. He also teaches illustration. When Shahar isn't illustrating, he enjoys the outdoors, taking care of his garden (which is very small as well!), and finding little insect friends there.

Parents, you can learn more about Shahar at SKober.com.

Hi, parents and caregivers,

We hope your child enjoyed *Children's Advent Stories for Bedtime*. If you have any questions or concerns about this book, or have received a damaged copy, please contact customerservice@penguinrandomhouse.com. We're here and happy to help.

Also, please consider writing a review on your favorite retailer's website to let others know what you and your child thought of the book!

Sincerely,
The Zeitgeist Team